How to Solve
Sudoku and Kakuro
A step-by-step introduction

$2/09 \sim S,$

First published in Great Britain in 2006 by
Allison & Busby Limited
13 Charlotte Mews
London W1T 4EJ
www.allisonandbusby.com

A catalogue record for this book is available from
the British Library.

10 9 8 7 6 5 4 3 2 1

ISBN 0 7490 8005 1
978-0-7490-8005-1

Printed and bound in Great Britain by
Bookmarque Ltd, Croydon, Surrey

Contents

Introduction

What are sudoku and kakuro? They are number games: puzzles that use only numbers, with all their infinite patterns and combinations. These are games for anyone and everyone; simple to learn, easy at first, and then, as the level advances, filled with astute tricks and numerical reasonings.

Unlike most mathematical puzzles, sudoku and kakuro use no words at all and no deeper mathematics than adding and combining small numbers. They can be simple enough to yield the restful feeling of numbers clicking smoothly into place, or they can contain levels beyond levels of logical reasoning, taxing the brain to the utmost. And, as millions of people are discovering, finding a solution invariably comes with a particularly marked sense of satisfaction and accomplishment. This feeling is so widespread and so strong that I believe that these puzzles are actually more than mere distractions; my feeling is that the profound interest and satisfaction displayed by their many adepts springs from the fact that in our social and professional lives – with the exception, of course, of certain very particular professions – the numerical talents of our brains are sadly underused. Sudoku and kakuro stimulate a part of the mind that lies dormant most of the time, and as such, they cannot but sharpen our minds and hone our too frequently rusty and neglected thinking and reasoning skills.

A newcomer to the puzzles may, however, be put off by

their difficulty. Many people – like myself – saw their first sudoku on the page of a newspaper, and quite possibly it was a shockingly difficult one, unsuitable and even discouraging for a first approach. The goal of this little book is to give an introduction to sudoku and kakuro by degrees, together with the main techniques and tricks for solving them. Here are not just rules to apply like a recipe, but something deeper; how to get a feel for the shape of the puzzles, where to look to have the best chance of finding yet another digit to slip into place, how to develop not just logical reasoning but also intuition and familiarity. Easy, medium and difficult examples are worked out in detail, illustrating each logical principle, and exercise puzzles for the reader, with hints – and the solutions at the end of the book – are provided at the end of each section to test understanding of each new rule. By the end of this book, the reader should be entirely capable of solving sudoku and kakuro at any level (and helping the people sitting next to one in the tube when they get stuck).

A last word, for those who are drawn to sudoku and kakuro by something more than just the pleasure of manipulating the logic and the numbers; those who wonder where such puzzles came from, and what the origin and history of number puzzles might be: this book also contains an appendix on magic squares, of which sudoku are merely a modern example. Magic squares are ancient, magic squares are extraordinary, as astonishing and varied as their name suggests. In all their different forms, they were believed by the ancients to have special powers. These forms, together with their fascinating history and the discoveries, little by little over centuries, of how to create and solve them, are presented in the appendix.

I would like to extend my grateful thanks to Vegard Hannsen, who, for the greater delight and amusement of the Norwegian and international population, has created gigantic websites

http://www.menneske.no/sudoku/eng

and

http://www.menneske.no/kakuro/eng

containing literally millions of freely available sudoku and kakuro puzzles with graded levels, which can be printed out or done online. Some of the puzzles in this book, particularly the more difficult kakuro, are reproduced from his collection with his permission.

Catherine Shaw

Chapter One – Sudoku

What is a sudoku?

It is simply a 9-by-9 grid of 81 cells, divided into nine 3-by-3 squares; the rows, columns and squares are numbered 1 to 9 as in the following diagram:

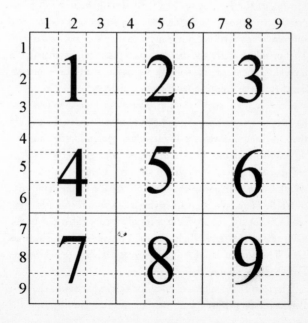

The puzzle is given with a few cells filled in with single digits (no zeros), and the goal is to fill out every cell with exactly one digit (no zeros) in such a way that: each row contains the digits 1 through 9, each column contains the digits 1 through 9, each square contains the digits 1 through 9.

In a proper sudoku (most published ones, in particular), there is never any guessing involved. Logical reasoning should provide a unique answer for *some* cell at every single step. One does occasionally come across a sudoku where, at some point, no cell contains a uniquely determined digit, and one is obliged to guess and go on from there until either the final solution or a contradiction is reached. But this is contrary to the true nature of sudoku, which is supposed to be a test of logic and rapidity, not luck.

One of the joys of sudoku is that even the most difficult puzzle is not *really* difficult; the techniques needed to solve sudoku of any level are not many, and they are easily mastered. The problem with the harder grids consists essentially in trying to locate a place in the sudoku grid where one or another of the solution techniques can apply.

Easy sudoku are characterised by the fact that just two basic solution techniques will solve them entirely. To explain these techniques, we need to introduce the notion of a *possible* digit and an *impossible* digit associated to a given cell. A digit is *impossible* for a given cell if it already appears in another cell which belongs either to the same square, or to the same row, or to the same column. Otherwise it is a *possible* digit for that cell. Obviously, as more and more digits are filled out in the grid, fewer and fewer digits become possible for the various cells. The goal of a sudoku is to successively spot cells where, for whatever reason, there is *only one* possible digit.

There are several basic rules for solving sudoku; the first two or three suffice for all easy or medium sudoku, and the subsequent ones apply only to the difficult or very difficult kind. Beyond the simple application of rules, there are two essential approaches to actually solving the puzzles.

Scanning. One studies the empty cells of the grid individually, searching for those which visibly can contain only a single possible digit. There are tips (see below) for looking at the most promising places right away rather than studying the cells in order.

Pencil marks. With a pencil (and according to the size of one's puzzle, on a copy) one can write tiny pencil marks at the top of each cell, showing the possible digits which can go in that cell. Then as digits are added to the puzzle, the pencil marks are erased, revealing new cells which must contain a single digit.

Guessing. In principle, guessing is against the spirit of sudoku, which is supposed to be solvable entirely by logical reasoning. However, it has been discovered that there are certain sudoku for which logical techniques, at least the known ones, simply do not suffice. Furthermore, guessing may actually sometimes lead to a solution more speedily than hunting idealistically for a difficult logical configuration in the possibilities. So we restrict ourselves here to a piece of advice: do your guesswork in pencil (!) and guess, when possible, in a cell that contains only two possibilities, so that if one guess leads to a contradiction, one may place the other possibility with confidence. If one guess only leads to a stuck position where another guess seems necessary, it is probably useless. The puzzle below is one of those which appear to require guessing, although known to possess a unique solution.

	6			7			3	
		3	5		1	7		
1	4		3		2		7	5
	8						9	
2	9		4		7		1	6
		2	8		5	1		
	3			2			5	

The scanning technique is much quicker and more efficient for easier puzzles. Medium or hard puzzles may require a combination of the two, with as much scanning accomplished as possible before, during and after the placement of the pencil marks. The very hardest puzzles will have few or no cells accessible to scanning, and pencil marks will be necessary almost from the beginning. They have the disadvantage that it takes time, patience and a lot of care to fill them in accurately. However, once they are there, solving even the most difficult sudoku can become quick and easy, with the busy work eliminated and the puzzle reduced to its most interesting logical elements.

Easy Sudoku

The easiest sudoku puzzles can be solved entirely by scanning, using just the two following basic rules.

Rule 1. Cells that can contain only one digit. Scan the puzzle for cells in which only a single digit is possible, and fill them in.

Rule 2. Digits that can go into only one cell (of a row, column or square). For each row (column, square), consider the digits not yet filled in to it. If any one of them appears as a possible in *only one* cell of that row (column, square), then it must be in that cell, and can be filled in.

For an illustration of rule 2, consider the following square (page 14) of a sudoku, where two digits (1 and 3) are already filled in, and the possible digits for each remaining cell are written in as tiny 'pencil marks'.

In this diagram, there is no cell which can contain only a single digit as in rule 1. In other words, there is no cell in which only a single digit appears as a pencil mark. However, there is one digit which can only go into a single cell, as per rule 2, namely the digit 5, which appears as a pencil mark only in the middle cell of the left-hand column. Since the 5 cannot go anywhere else in the square, it must go there; it can be filled in. If there are other pencil marks in the grid, then all the 5's appearing as pencil marks in the same row and column can be erased.

278	26	
		1
456	489	247
468		679
	3	

→

278	26	
		1
5	489	247
468		679
	3	

Speed tips for rapid scanning: Every cell can be checked individually to see whether by chance it can be filled out either by rule 1 or by rule 2. So the only question is, what is the best place to start looking, and which digits should be considered first. The tip for digits is: *first consider digits of which several already appear in the grid*, and this tip of course remains valid at any stage of the puzzle. The tip for cells is: *first check all the cells belonging to rows, columns, or squares that already contain several digits*, and, even better, start with the cells that are in intersections of such rows, columns and squares.

A very easy sudoku

			1		4	7	3	
2	3	6	7					
	1		5	6			9	
				1	6	8		3
7		8					9	2
1		3	9	8				
	5			7	2		8	
					9	6	5	1
	8	4	6		1			

For instance, in our puzzle, one good place to inspect first – obviously there are many possible ways to solve a sudoku – would be the fourth column of the grid, which already contains five digits. The missing digits in this column are 2, 3, 4 and 8. The places for the 2, the 3 and the 4 are not uniquely determined. However, the 8 can only go in the lowest empty cell of the column, the second-to-last cell, since placing it in any of the other empty cells of the fourth column would give either two 8's in the same row or two 8's in the same square. Now that the 8 is in place, there is only a unique cell where the 2 can go, namely the fourth from the top.

Another good column to look at is the sixth, which also has five digits. The missing digits are 3, 5, 7 and 8. Here, we find that there is only one cell of the column, namely the sixth cell from the top, which can contain the 7. Then there is only a unique cell which can contain the 5, namely the cell just above the 7.

Now let us consider squares. Square 2 has five digits, and there is only one cell which can contain the 2, then the 3, after which also the 8 and the 9 appear automatically and the square is complete.

Square 5 already contains seven digits but it is not yet possible to determine where to place the missing 3 and 4.

Square 8 has six digits and it is possible to place the missing 5, although not yet the 3 or the 4.

Let us consider rows now. Although the first and second rows contain several digits, there are none that can be placed. However the 2 in the third row can be placed, then the 7. In the fourth row nothing can be placed, but in the fifth row the 1 and the 6 can be placed, and in the sixth row the 2 can be placed, in the seventh row the 1, the 6 and the 9, in the eighth row the 4, the 7, the 2 and the 3 can be placed (in that order), completing the row, and finally, in the ninth row the 2, the 7 and the 9 can be placed, completing the row.

			1	2	4	7	3	
2	3	6	7	9	8			
	1	7	5	6	3	2	9	
			2	1	6	8		3
7	6	8			5	9	1	2
1	2	3	9	8	7			
6	5	1		7	2		8	9
3	7	2	8	4	9	6	5	1
9	8	4	6	5	1	3	2	7

This brings us to the final stage of the puzzle, in which there is nothing more to do than to rapidly complete the successive rows, columns and squares which are already almost full. Squares 2 and 7 are full, squares 8 and 9 lack only a single digit which can be immediately inserted. Square 5 lacks only the 3 and the 4 which can now be placed. The 4, the 8, the 5 and the 9 can be placed to complete square 1, then the 4, 5 and 9 of square 4. The first and third rows now lack only a single digit which can be placed. The 1, the 5 and the 4 now complete square 3, and finally, the 4, the 5, the 6 and the 7 are can be placed in square 6. The grid is complete.

8	9	5	1	2	4	7	3	6
2	3	6	7	9	8	1	4	5
4	1	7	5	6	3	2	9	8
5	4	9	2	1	6	8	7	3
7	6	8	4	3	5	9	1	2
1	2	3	9	8	7	5	6	4
6	5	1	3	7	2	4	8	9
3	7	2	8	4	9	6	5	1
9	8	4	6	5	1	3	2	7

A fairly easy sudoku

		2	4		9		6	
6								
		5	6		2			3
5		4		2	8	3		9
			3		1			
1		3	5	6		8		2
3			2		5	6		8
	2		9		6		4	

This puzzle is more complicated than the previous one, but the same two rules and the same scanning tips end up conquering it.

Again we scan for rows, columns and squares with many digits rather than studying every row in order. We start with the fourth and sixth rows. The fourth row looks promising, and indeed the 1, the 6 and the 7 can be added to it immediately, completing it. The 4 can be added to the sixth row. Now the middle square lacks only its final 9, which we add. The sixth column also lacks only a single digit, the 7 in square 8. The fourth column lacks only two digits, but they cannot be determined yet.

Instead of testing the remaining rows, columns and

squares, which are less full, let us use the other technique and consider the digits of which several are already present in the grid. There are already seven 6's in the grid, and we easily place the remaining two (in squares 6 and 7). There are six 2's in the grid, and we can place the 2 in square 4, although the 2's in squares 3 and 9 remain undetermined. There are five 3's in the grid, which is enough to allow us to place the 3 in square 9, then the one in square 8, then the one in square 2 and finally the one in square 1, so that all the 3's are now present. Furthermore, this now makes it possible to complete the 2's. Indeed, the 2 in square 9 is now determined (since a 3 now occupies one of the two possible cells it could have occupied previously), which then also lets us determine the 2 in square 3. The 2's, 3's and 6's are now completely finished.

	3	2	4		9		6	
6					3		2	
		5	6		2			3
5	6	4	7	2	8	3	1	9
2			3	9	1			6
1		3	5	6	4	8		2
3			2		5	6		8
		6			7	2	3	
	2		9	3	6		4	

Now some rows, squares and columns have become much fuller than they were before, so let's consider them. Square 6 has six digits and we can place the 4, then the 5 and the 7, completing it. Then we can add the missing 9 to complete the sixth row. Square 4 is almost full but the remaining two digits cannot be placed. Neither can anything be added to square 8. So let us try the rows, columns and squares containing 5 digits. The 9 can be placed in square 9, and the missing 8 can now be placed to complete the eighth column.

Note that we now have six 9's in the grid, so it is worth looking for the others, and indeed, we can add the 9 in square 7, then the 9 in square 1, and finally the one in square 3, completing the 9's.

	3	2	4		9		6	
6		9			3		2	
		5	6		2	9	8	3
5	6	4	7	2	8	3	1	9
2			3	9	1	4	5	6
1	9	3	5	6	4	8	7	2
3			2		5	6	9	8
9		6			7	2	3	
	2		9	3	6		4	

The first column has six digits, and we can place the 4. Now there are six 4's in the grid, and this helps place a seventh one, namely the one in square 3, although the 4's in squares 7 and 8 are still undetermined. There are five 5's in the grid, and we find that we can place the one in square 7, which now makes it possible to go back and place the 4 in square 7 and then the 4 in square 8. The complete digits in the puzzle are now 2, 3, 4, 6 and 9.

Now the most promising place to look is square 8, which lacks only two digits, and indeed we can complete it by placing the 1 and the 8. We then add the 1 to complete the fourth column. Since we now have five 1's in the puzzle, we check if we can now place any more, and find that the 1 in the second column now appears, then the 1 in the third column, then the 1 in the seventh and finally the 1 in the ninth column, completing the 1's.

	3	2	4		9	1	6	
6		9	1		3		2	4
4	1	5	6		2	9	8	3
5	6	4	7	2	8	3	1	9
2			3	9	1	4	5	6
1	9	3	5	6	4	8	7	2
3	4		2	1	5	6	9	8
9	5	6	8	4	7	2	3	1
	2	1	9	3	6		4	

We are now entering the final stage of the puzzle, where virtually everything is completed by adding one final digit. We add the 7 to complete the seventh row, then the 8 to complete square 7, the 7 to complete the first column, the 8 to complete the third column, the 8 to complete square 1, the 7 to complete square 4, and the 7 to complete the third row. A 5 and an 8 are missing in square 2 but the 8 can now be placed, then the 5; a 5 then completes the first row and a 7 completes the second, a 5 completes the seventh column and a 7 the ninth. The puzzle is done.

7	3	2	4	8	9	1	6	5
6	8	9	1	5	3	7	2	4
4	1	5	6	7	2	9	8	3
5	6	4	7	2	8	3	1	9
2	7	8	3	9	1	4	5	6
1	9	3	5	6	4	8	7	2
3	4	7	2	1	5	6	9	8
9	5	6	8	4	7	2	3	1
8	2	1	9	3	6	5	4	7

And finally...an easy sudoku for the reader

Hint: start with 1's and 8's.

8								1
		2	7		9	4		
		1		8		3		
	8			5			9	
		6	4		8	5		
	1			3			6	
		4		6		9		
		7	5		1	8		
9								7

Medium Sudoku

The new rules and techniques we introduce in this section and the next one differ from the basic rules 1 and 2 in that they do not actually allow one to fill any new digits into the grid, but allow one to eliminate *possible* numbers from the cells, thereby sometimes yielding new cells that can contain only a single digit. The first speed tip is a refinement of the principle of considering digits which appear many times in the grid.

Speed tip: Instead of considering the digits of which a large number already appear, one can consider those of which a 'large number', namely two out of three, appear in *one third* of the grid, either in one of the three rows of squares or in one of the three columns of squares. If two out of three digits appear in one row (or column) of squares, then it is sometimes possible to place the third one.

Rule 3. Twin pairs. A twin pair is a pair of cells in the same row (or column, or square) containing only two identical possibles. For instance, if you have two cells in the same row, both of which contain only 1 and 4 as possibles, that is a twin pair. The point is that if you have such a pair in a row (or column, or square), then the digits 1 and 4 must go into those two cells, although you may not yet know which digit goes into which cell. But in any case those two digits cannot go into any other cell of the row (column, square), and this should be taken into account when calculating the possible digits that can go into a given cell.

27	26	1
245 6	489	247
246 8	3	27

→

27	6	1
456	489	4
468	3	27

Note that even when it seems that two cells of a given square (row, column) contain many possibles, they actually form a twin pair when in fact there are two digits which only appear among the possibles for those two cells and no others of the same square (row, column). This means that the two digits must fit into those two cells, and all the other seeming possibles of those cells are actually impossible.

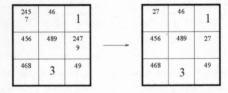

245 7	46	1
456	489	247 9
468	3	49

→

27	46	1
456	489	27
468	3	49

Rule 3a. Triples. A *triple* is a set of three cells in the same row (or column, or square) containing three possibles distributed between them in any way. For instance, if you have three cells in the same row (column, square), containing the possibles '379', '379', '79' or '24', '26', '46', then that is a triple. You may not yet know where each of the three digits goes, but you can be sure that they must go into these three cells. Therefore they cannot go into any of the other cells of the row (column, square) and can be eliminated from the 'possible' digits for that cell. In the following diagram, for instance, the triple 278, 28 and 78 eliminates those possibles from all the other cells of the square.

278	28	1
456	489	247
78	3	679

→

278	28	1
5	49	
78	3	69

Rule 3b. Quadruples. The same rule works with a *quadruple* of numbers in four cells, although this is rather rarely useful in practice.

267 89	28	1
5	489	248
246 8	3	289

→

7	28	1
5	489	248
6	3	289

Rule 4. Twins (and triples etc.) in intersections. Every time twins, triples, quadruples etc. occur in a grid, they should be considered also with respect to the squares, rows and columns intersecting the one where they occur. If a twin pair that occurs in a square, for instance, also belongs to a row, then the digits of the pair can be erased from all the possibilities in the square *and* in the row. If a triple appearing for example in square 1 shows that the 9 in square 1 must appear in the first column of the grid, then this means that the 9 in the first column must appear in square 1, so the 9 can be erased from the pencil marks in the rest of the first column.

Rule 4a. Regions. More generally, it can be very useful to keep account of digits which are necessarily in a certain *region* of a given row, square or column (whether or not they appear as part of a twin, triple or quadruple) to erase them as possibilities from the other cells of that row, square or column.

		1				6		
		9				2		
		6	1	2	9	3		
	6			5			3	
	9		7		3		2	
	3			9			7	
		5	8	7	1	9		
		7				8		
		3				7		

For instance, in the sudoku above, the 3 in square 9 cannot lie in columns seven or eight, so it must lie in column nine, but at first, we don't know where in column nine it should be placed. However, noticing that the 3 in square 7 is in the bottom row (row nine), we see that since the top row of square 8 is full, the 3 cannot lie in it, nor can it lie in the bottom row which already contains a 3 (in square 7), therefore the 3 in square 8 lies in the middle row of the square (eighth row). Thus, we now know that the 3 in square 9 lies in the top row of the square (row seven) and can place it!

Rule 4b. Using regions to eliminate possibilities. The same rule can make it possible to erase possibilities, even without placing new numbers. For instance, in the diagram below, we see that since the 5 is in the top row of the left-hand square, it cannot be in the top row of the middle square, nor can it be in the middle row of the middle square since that row is full. So the 5 in the middle square necessarily lies in the bottom row of that square. Therefore, the 5 in the right-hand square cannot lie in the top or in the bottom row, so it must lie in the middle row. And even if 5's appear in the possibilities of the three cells in the bottom row of the right-hand square, we can erase them by this reasoning.

	5					3		9
			7	1	6			
	2					5̸	5̸	5̸

Let us now work through three example sudokus which make increasing use of these new rules.

A sudoku with twins

	6		2		7			
	1							
	9	2		3		1		
	3	4			6	5	2	
7		6				4		8
1			5					7
		5		9		6		
						7	9	3
			7		8			

Start by considering the 7's. Because there are two 7's in the second row of squares (squares 4, 5 and 6), we can try to add in the missing 7 in square 5, and indeed it is uniquely determined! So is the 7 in square 7, and we then obtain the 7 in square 1, then the 7 in square 3.

In the second row of squares of the grid there are also two 6's (in squares 4 and 5), and in fact the third one can be placed in square 6. Also, there are already two 5's in the same row of squares, and we can place the third 5, in square 4. Then we note that in the top row of squares there are two 1's, and we can place the third 1 in square 2. (There are other places to consider: two 4's in the second row of squares, two 9's in the third row, two 1's and also two 5's and two 6's in the first column of squares (squares 1, 4 and 7), two 6's in the third column of squares (squares 3, 6 and 9), which do not give a result yet but can be considered again later.)

Now let us consider nearly full rows, columns and squares.

Square 4 contains six digits. None of the three empty cells seems to contain only one possible digit. But here is a place where the twin pair rule applies. We write the possible digits as pencil marks in each of the three empty cells of square 4.

	6		2	1	7			
	1	7						
	9	2		3		1	7	
89	3	4		7	6	5	2	
7	5	6				4		8
1	28	89	5				6	7
	7	5		9		6		
						7	9	3
			7		8			

There are two cells which can only contain an 8 or a 9; they form a twin pair, and the 8 and the 9 of square 4 must lie in those two cells. Therefore, by rule 3, the remaining cell which apparently has 2 and 8 as possibilities really can only contain a 2, which we place.

This now leaves only two empty cells at the bottom of the second column. Two empty cells in a row, column or square always form a twin pair – except, of course, when the two numbers can actually be placed, which is the case here, since an 8 cannot lie in the bottom row. So the 4 lies there and the 8 just above, completing the second column.

Now there are two 8's in the last row of squares, in square 7 and in square 8, and we find that we can place the 8 in square 9. Square 9 now contains five digits, so it's natural to have a closer look, and we discover that the 2 can be placed in it. Let us pencil mark the possibilities for the remaining three empty cells. We find a twin pair 15-15, and another cell with possibilities 14.

	6		2	1	7			
	1	7						
	9	2		3		1	7	
89	3	4		7	6	5	2	
7	5	6				4		8
1	2	89	5				6	7
	7	5		9		6	8	14
	8					7	9	3
	4		7		8	2	15	15

Because of rule 3, the 14 cell must contain the 4! We cannot place the 1 and the 5 yet, but note that there are now two 2's in the third column of squares (squares 3, 6 and 9) and we can place the third one in square 3.

Now, because the new twin pair is in the last row, it is natural to see if it helps complete the last row. We pencil mark the possibilities for the empty cells in the last row.

	6		2	1	7			
	1	7						2
	9	2		3		1	7	
89 / 3	4		7	6	5	2		
7	5	6				4		8
1	2	89	5				6	7
	7	5		9		6	8	4
	8					7	9	3
369 / 4	139	7	56	8	2	15	15	

By rule 3, the cell containing only 56 as possibilities actually must contain the 6, and the cell containing possibilities 139 actually can only contain 3 or 9. The new 6 in square 8 means that the last row of squares now contains two 6's, and we can place the third one, in square 7. The pencil marks in the lowest left-hand cell can now be reduced to 3 and 9. Square

7 now contains five digits, so we take a closer look towards completing it, and find that we can place the 1, then the 2, although the two empty cells still constitute a twin pair 39-39.

The seventh row now has only two empty cells, which form a twin pair 13-13 in square 8. This limits the possibilities for the remaining three empty cells of square 8, so we test them and find that we can place the 4 in square 8, and the two remaining cells form a twin pair 25-25.

Our puzzle is now equipped with five different twin pairs; what sometimes happens in such situations is that a single digit, placed later on, settles just one twin pair and then, like dominos, they settle each other successively all over the grid. So it is extremely useful to keep the twin pair pencil marks visible.

	6		2	1	7			
	1	7						2
	9	2		3		1	7	
89 3		4		7	6	5	2	
7	5	6				4		8
1	2	89	5				6	7
2	7	5	13	9	13	6	8	4
6	8	1	4	25	25	7	9	3
39	4	39	7	6	8	2	15	15

Recall that earlier, we noted that there were two 4's in the second row of squares, two 9's in the third row, two 1's and also two 5's and two 6's in the first column of squares (squares 1, 4 and 7), and two 6's in the third column of squares (squares 3, 6 and 9), none of which allowed us to fill in the third one. Let us pick up these pairs again for a fresh look. Some yield nothing new and others are already done, but the two 6's in the third column of squares now allows us to place the third one, in square 3. We now have two 6's in the first row of squares and we can place the third one, in square 2. Now there are five digits in square 2, so we take a closer look, and find that we can place the 9, then the 8. The remaining two cells contain a new 45-45 twin pair. The new 8 gives two 8's in the second column of squares, and we can now place the one in square 5.

	6		2	1	7			
	1	7	6	45	9			2
	9	2	8	3	45	1	7	6
89	3	4		7	6	5	2	
7	5	6				4		8
1	2	89	5	8			6	7
2	7	5	13	9	13	6	8	4
6	8	1	4	25	25	7	9	3
39	4	39	7	6	8	2	15	15

A very pleasing thing now happens. The new 8 gives two 8's in the second row of squares, determining the 8 in square 4, settling the 89-89 twin pair in square 4 and the 39-39 twin pair in square 7. Then we can place the 8 at the top of the third column, completing it. There are now eight 8's in the grid, and we can place the final one, in square 3. This leaves only two empty cells in the seventh column, and they can be filled by placing first the 3 in square 6, then the 9 in square 3. Now we can add the missing 1 and 9 in square 6, completing it, and this settles the 15-15 twin pair at the bottom of the puzzle. We can add the 5 at the top of the ninth column, completing it. Square 3 is now almost complete, containing just two empty cells which form a 34-34 twin pair.

3	6	8	2	1	7	9	4	5
5	1	7	6	4	9	8	3	2
4	9	2	8	3	5	1	7	6
8	3	4	1	7	6	5	2	9
7	5	6	9	2	3	4	1	8
1	2	9	5	8	4	3	6	7
2	7	5	3	9	1	6	8	4
6	8	1	4	5	2	7	9	3
9	4	3	7	6	8	2	5	1

We add the missing 4 to complete the sixth row, which settles the 45-45 twin pair in square 2, and then the 25-25 twin pair in square 8. Then we add the missing 1 to complete the fourth row, which settles the 13-13 twin pair in square 8. Then we add the 9 to complete the fourth column, then the 2 and the 3 to complete square 5. Finally, we add the 4 to complete the third row. Then we can place the missing 5, then the 3, in square 1, settling the last 34-34 twin pair in square 3. The puzzle is done.

A more complicated sudoku with twins

							6	3
4	5	2						
			7	9	4			
			5			9		4
		4		3		1		
7		8		6				
			6	7	8			
						6	5	2
1	4							

We begin by considering the rows of squares and columns of squares containing two of the same digit, as indicated in the speed tip at the beginning of this section. We find no less than seven new digits this way:

- Two 6's in the third row of squares determine the 6 in square 7

- Two 6's in the third column of squares determine the 6 in square 6

- Two 6's in the second column of squares determine the 6 in square 2

- Two 4's in the first row of squares determine the 4 in square 3

- Two 4's in the second row of squares determine the 4 in square 5

- Two 4's in the second column of squares determine the 4 in square 8

- Two 4's in the third row of squares determine the 4 in square 9

Note that all the 4's are now placed in the grid.

Now, continuing with our basic techniques, we consider the fifth column of the grid, which already contains six digits. We find that the bottom cell of this column can only contain a 2. The two empty cells at the top of this column form a twin pair with possibilities 18-18.

Now consider the ninth column, which has five digits. We find that the sixth cell from the top can only contain a 5. This then gives two 5's in the third column of squares, which determine the 5 in square 3. We also have two 5's in the second row of squares, which determine the 5 in square 4.

Now consider the seventh column, which contains five digits. We find that the seventh cell of this column must contain a 3. Then the cell just above it must contain a 2. We complete this column with a 78-78 twin pair.

Now the seventh row contains six digits, and only the final cell can contain the missing 1. We complete it with a 29-29 twin pair.

The sixth row contains six digits. The missing digits are 1, 3 and 9. Clearly only the 3 can go into the eighth cell. We complete the row with a 19-19 twin pair.

The fifth row contains five digits, so it's worth checking, but no useful digits or twin pairs appear.

Let us complete square 6 with its 78-78 twin pair.

						4	6	3
4	5	2			6			
			7	9	4			
				5		9		4
		4		3		1		6
7		8	4	6				
			6	7	8		4	
				4		6	5	2
1	4	6						

				18		4	6	3
4	5	2		18	6	78		
			7	9	4	5		
				5		9	78	4
5		4		3		1	78	6
7	19	8	4	6	19	2	3	5
29	29	5	6	7	8	3	4	1
				4		6	5	2
1	4	6		2		78		

Now, where a twin pair lies in a given row, column or square, one can try to fill out that row, column or square exactly as if the twin pair of cells already contained determined numbers; regardless of the fact that we don't know which of the twin numbers goes in which cell of the pair, we know that no other number goes in either one of the twin cells. From this point of view, square 2 can be considered as containing six digits (with its twin pair 18-18), and we find since there is already a 3 in the top row and there cannot be one in the twin pair, there is only one cell where the 3 can be placed in square 2. Then we can also place the 2 in square 2.

We can treat the eighth column, with its twin pair 78-78, in the same way, and we find that there is only one cell where the 2 can go, then only one cell where the 1 can go, which allows us to place the 9 at the bottom, and complete square 9 with a

78-78 twin pair. This means that the ninth row contains the same 78-78 twin pair, so we try to complete it and find that we can place the missing 3 and 5. Square 8 can now be completed with a 19-19 twin pair.

Since the sixth column contains four digits and a twin pair, we try to complete it and find that there is only one cell where the 5 can go, and the remaining two empty cells form a 27-27 twin pair.

			2	18	5	4	6	3
4	5	2	3	18	6	78	1	
			7	9	4	5	2	
				5	27	9	78	4
5		4		3	27	1	78	6
7	19	8	4	6	19	2	3	5
29	29	5	6	7	8	3	4	1
			19	4	19	6	5	2
1	4	6	5	2	3	78	9	78

Let us try to complete the ninth column which has six digits. Only 7, 8 and 9 are missing, and we see now that only 8 can lie in the third cell. So the lowest cell, which belongs to a 78-78 twin pair, must contain 7 and the second cell of the ninth column contains the 9, whereas the 78-78 twin pair in square 9 is now also resolved. We can also place the final missing 7 in square 3, then the missing 8 in the second row, resolving the 18-18 twin pair in square 2.

Since the third column contains five digits, let us try to complete it. We find that while we cannot place any digits, the four empty cells form two twin pairs, a 13-13 pair and a 79-79 pair.

		79	2	1	5	4	6	3
4	5	2	3	8	6	7	1	9
		13	7	9	4	5	2	8
		13		5	27	9	78	4
5		4		3	27	1	78	6
7	19	8	4	6	19	2	3	5
29	29	5	6	7	8	3	4	1
		79	19	4	19	6	5	2
1	4	6	5	2	3	8	9	7

Now consider the eighth row. It already contains a 19-19 twin pair, and now its third cell contains the possibilities 7 and 9. From the twin pair rule 3, this third cell must contain 7, resolving the 79-79 twin pair of the third column. We complete the eighth row with a 38-38 twin pair.

Only the first two cells are empty now in the first row, and instead of forming a twin pair, we find that they can be placed, completing the first row.

At this point there are so few empty cells that we complete all of the pencil marks.

8	7	9	2	1	5	4	6	3
4	5	2	3	8	6	7	1	9
36	136	13	7	9	4	5	2	8
236	1236	13	18	5	27	9	78	4
5	29	4	89	3	27	1	78	6
7	19	8	4	6	19	2	3	5
29	29	5	6	7	8	3	4	1
38	38	7	19	4	19	6	5	2
1	4	6	5	2	3	8	9	7

We perceive a 29-29 twin pair in the second column, which forces a 1 in the sixth cell of that column by the twin pair rule, resolving the 19-19 twin pair in the sixth row. This then forces the 8 and the 1 in square 5. Then we find the 3 in the fourth row, resolving the 13-13 twin pair in the third column.

There is only one place where the 8 can go in the second column, so we place it, resolving the 38-38 twin pair in square 7. This then determines the 6 in the first column, then the 3 in square 1, the 6 in the second column, then the 2 and the 9 in square 4, resolving the 29-29 twin pair in the second column, and the 29-29 twin pair in square 7.

Since there is now a 2 in the fourth row, the sixth cell of that row must be 7 and the eighth cell 8, completing the row. This also resolves the 27-27 twin pair of square 5 and the 78-78 twin pair of square 6. Finally, we solve the 19-19 twin pair of square 8. The puzzle is done.

8	7	9	2	1	5	4	6	3
4	5	2	3	8	6	7	1	9
6	3	1	7	9	4	5	2	8
2	6	3	1	5	7	9	8	4
5	9	4	8	3	2	1	7	6
7	1	8	4	6	9	2	3	5
9	2	5	6	7	8	3	4	1
3	8	7	9	4	1	6	5	2
1	4	6	5	2	3	8	9	7

A sudoku with twins, triples and quadruples

	2						9	
4				6				1
	7		1		9		4	
		4		5	8	1		
	9		7		3		2	
		2	6	9		5		
	4		8		1		6	
6				3				4
	8						1	

Just a quick glance at the start of this puzzle shows that the top half of the puzzle, at least, is fairly peopled by 9's, and indeed we can immediately add the 9 in the second row and the 9 in the fourth row, although the last three rows remain without 9's. The puzzle also contains no less than five 1's, all towards the right side of the grid, making it possible to quickly add the 1 in square 5, although not those in the three leftmost columns. Square 5 is now nearly full, and we add the 4 and then the 2 to complete it. Now the grid contains six 4's, and we can add the one in square 6. There are only four 6's in the grid, but it's worth a glance; we find that we can place the 6 in square 8, the one in square 6 and the one in square 4.

Now the puzzle is stuck, the basic methods no longer yield any digits. In order to explain the continuation, we add pencil marks to each cell, containing the possible digits which can go there.

135 8	2	135 68	345	478	57	367 8	9	357 8
4	35	9	35	6	257	237 8	357 8	1
358	7	356 8	1	28	9	236 8	4	235 8
37	6	4	2	5	8	1	37	9
58	9	58	7	1	3	4	2	6
137	13	2	6	9	4	5	378	378
235 79	4	357	8	27	1	237 9	6	235 7
6	15	157	59	3	257	278 9	578	4
235 79	8	357	459	247	6	237 9	1	235 7

Our goal is now to reduce the possibilities in some cells using rules 3, 4 and 5. For example, the twin pair 35-35 in the second row means that the 3 and the 5 must go in those two cells, so the pencil marks 257, 2378, 3578 in the remaining empty cells of the second row become just 27, 278, 78. There is a quadruple with the digits 1, 3, 5, 7 in square 7, so we can remove these possibilities from the other two empty cells in square 7 (the two empty cells in the first column), obtaining just a 29-29 twin pair.

There are still no cells which can only contain a single digit, but quickly scanning the pencil-marked puzzle to see if there are any rows, columns or squares in which some digit can only go into one place now yields the 5 in the eighth column!

1358	2	13568	345	478	57	3678	9	3578
4	35	9	35	6	27	278	78	1
358	7	3568	1	28	9	2368	4	2358
37	6	4	2	5	8	1	37	9
58	9	58	7	1	3	4	2	6
137	13	2	6	9	4	5	378	378
29	4	357	8	27	1	2379	6	2357
6	15	157	59	3	257	2789	5	4
29	8	357	459	247	6	2379	1	2357

The new 5 then successively determines the 1, the 7, the 9, the 2 and the 8 in the eighth row, completing it. Each of these new digits must be inspected to see if it has something to offer in terms of new forced numbers, in the square and column that it lives in. The new 1 determines the 3 and the 5 in the second column, completing it. The new 2 determines the 7 and the 5 in the sixth column, completing it, and it also determines the 7, then the 4 and the 5 in square 8, completing that. The new 3 in square 4 determines the 7 in square 4, then the 1 in square 4.

The new 5 in square 8 determines the 3 and then the 4 at the top of the fourth column, completing that. Then the 8 and the 2 can be added to square 2, completing it. The pencil marks then allow us to determine the 2 and the 8 in the second row, completing that. Then we place the 7 and the 3 in the eighth column, completing it, and the missing 8 in square 6, completing that. We can also now place the 3 and the 5 in square 7, settling one twin pair. This then determines the 8 in the third column.

We now renew the pencil marks according to all the new digits.

38 2	136	4	8	5	367 9	37
4	5	9	3	6	7	2	8	1
38 7	36	1	2	9	36 4	35
7	6	4	2	5	8	1	3	9
58 9	8	7	1	3	4	2	6
1	3	2	6	9	4	5	7	8
29 4	5	8	7	1	39 6	23
6	1	7	9	3	2	8	5	4
29 8	3	5	4	6	379 1	237

Back to the basic techniques, there is a unique cell in the third row where the 5 can go and a unique cell where the 8 can go. This 8 determines the 3 and the 5 in the first column. Then we place the 6 and the 1 in square 1, completing it. This determines the 3, then the 7, then the 6 in square 3, completing that. Finally, the 9 and the 7 are determined in the seventh column, then the 2 and the 3 there, and finally the 29-29 twin pair in square 7 is settled. The puzzle is done.

3	2	1	4	8	5	6	9	7
4	5	9	3	6	7	2	8	1
8	7	6	1	2	9	3	4	5
7	6	4	2	5	8	1	3	9
5	9	8	7	1	3	4	2	6
1	3	2	6	9	4	5	7	8
2	4	5	8	7	1	9	6	3
6	1	7	9	3	2	8	5	4
9	8	3	5	4	6	7	1	2

And finally...a medium sudoku for the reader

3				7				6
4		5		3		9		7
	7						5	
			8	9	3			
1	2		7		6		3	9
			1	5	2			
	9						7	
7		6		8		1		5
2				6				8

Difficult Sudoku

Difficult sudoku use a variety of other, more complicated rules to eliminate pencil-marked possibilities from the empty cells. These rules apply when the grid has reached the stage where basic scanning, twin pairs, etc. no longer give any new digits, and it becomes necessary to pencil mark the possibilities for each empty cell in the grid before seeking to apply them.

Rule 5. XY-wing This configuration comes up rather rarely. However it is worth looking for whenever a puzzle is stuck, but has several cells containing only two possibilities. The trick is to look for three cells (let's call them A, B and C) such that the possibilities contained in the three cells are ab, bc and ac, and cell A and cell B are in the same row while cell C is in the same column or in the same square as cell A, or else cell A and cell B are in the same column while cell C is in the same row or the same square as cell A.

⟋	ab a	⟋		bc b	
	ac c		⟋	⟋	⟋

In this situation, cell A is the pivot cell connected to both of the others. If cell A is actually the digit a, then cell C must contain c, whereas if cell A is actually the digit b, then cell B must contain c. In other words, whatever the real digit contained in A, either B or C is going to contain c. Therefore, any cell which simultaneously 'sees' both B and C (i.e. any cell which is in the same row, column or square as B and in the same row, column or square as C) cannot contain c as a possibility, and c can be erased from the pencil marks of all these squares.

This diagram shows two different types of XY-wing formation. In the top one, the pivot cell A contains the digits 25 in the same row as cell B containing 35 and in the same square as cell C containing 23 as possibilities. The cells which can 'see' both cell B and cell C are those which are in the same row as cell B and the same square as cell C and those which are in the same row as cell C and the same square as cell B, since the column of cell B does not intersect the square of cell C and vice versa, and the two squares are also disjoint. There are five cells which can 'see' both cell B and cell C, and none of them can contain 3 as a possibility. The lower example of XY-wing shows cell A in the same row as cell B and in the same column as cell C, but all three cells in different squares. In this formation, there is only one cell which can 'see' both cell A and cell B.

A sudoku using XY-wing

	1			4				2
	9	3						
	7			6	8			
		8				3	2	1
		9		3	5		8	
			8		6			
				1	3	5		6
5								
							1	8

We start by considering digits which appear frequently: the two 1's in the third row of squares yield the 1 in square 7, and the two 8's in the second column of squares yield the 8 in square 3. There is only one 8 in the first column of squares, but since the 8 in square 1 is necessarily in the first column, and the 8 in square 4 is in the third column, as explained in rule 4a, the 8 in square 7 must be in the second column, and therefore its position is uniquely determined.

	1			4				2
	9	3						
	7			6	8			
		8				3	2	1
		9		3	5		8	
			8		6			
	8			1	3	5		6
5		1		8				
							1	8

Now let us turn to scanning the rows, columns and squares with many digits to find digits which can only go into a single cell. The fifth column and the seventh row, although promising with their five digits, yield nothing. Let us consider the columns with four digits. The second column yields nothing but the sixth column contains only one cell where the 1 can go. The ninth column yields nothing, but the fourth row contains only one cell where the 5 can go. The fifth row yields nothing. Let us consider squares with four digits. Squares 1, 2, 3 and 4 yield nothing, but in square 5, there is only one cell where the 1 can go, then only one cell where the 2 can go, and this reflects back on square 4, where there is now only one cell where the 1 can go, then only one cell where the 3 can go. In square 6, there is only one cell where the 6 can go, which together with the 6 in square 5 now determines the 6 in square 4, and this then determines the 6 in square 1, then the 6 in square 3. Square 9 yields nothing. However, now the two 3's in the first column of squares gives the 3 in square 7, and then the two 9's in the first column of squares determine the 9 in square 7. We add the pencil marks as we go along to every square or row or column that lacks only three digits.

	1	6		4				2
	9	3		57	1	·	6	
	7			6	8			
6	5	8	479	79	479	3	2	1
247	24	9	1	3	5	6	8	47
1	3	247	8	2	6			
9	8	247	247	1	3	5	47	6
5	246	1		8				
3	246	247		579			1	8

55

A little further scanning at the top of the puzzle now shows that with all the new digits, the top left-hand cell of square 1 can only contain an 8. Then the two 8's in the first row of squares determines the 8 in square 3, and furthermore the 5 in square 1 is now determined. The two empty cells in square 1 form a 24-24 twin pair, so that by the twin pair rule, the fifth cell of the first column, which contained 247 as possibilities, must contain the 7. This determines the 4 and then the 2 in the fifth row, completing it. The three empty cells in the lowest row of square 6 contain the triple 79, 579, 579, showing that the third cell of the sixth row must contain the 4. This converts the pencil marks in square 7 to a 27-27 twin pair and a 46-46 twin pair.

Back to basic scanning, we note that the two 1's in the top row of squares determine the 1 in square 3, then that the 4 in square 3 is determined.

8	1	6		4				2
24 9		3		57	1	8	6	
24 7		5		6	8	1	4	
6	5	8	479	79	479	3	2	1
7	2	9	1	3	5	6	8	4
1	3	4	8	2	6	79	579	579
9	8	27	247	1	3	5	47	6
5	46 1			8				
3	46	27		579			1	8

The two 4's in the first row of squares then determines the 4 in square 1, resolving the 24-24 twin pair there. The two 2's, now in the first row of squares, determine the 2 in square 2. Finally, at this point, let us complete the grid with its pencil marks.

8	1	6	3579	4	79	79	3579	2
4	9	3	2	57	1	8	6	57
2	7	5	39	6	8	1	4	39
6	5	8	479	79	479	3	2	1
7	2	9	1	3	5	6	8	4
1	3	4	8	2	6	79	579	579
9	8	27	47	1	3	5	47	6
5	46	1	4679	8	2479	2479	379	379
3	46	27	45679	579	2479	2479	1	8

The 79-79 twin pair in the seventh column reduces the last two cells to a 24-24 twin pair. This in turn determines the 7 in square 9, reducing the other two empty cells to a 39-39 twin pair, which clears out the 9's from the possibilities in the empty cells of the eighth row. The 7 also determines the 2 and the 4 in the seventh row. This determines the 7 at the bottom of the third column. There is now only one place in square 5 where the 4 can go.

8	1	6	35	4	79	79	35	2
4	9	3	2	57	1	8	6	57
2	7	5	39	6	8	1	4	39
6	5	8	79	79	4	3	2	1
7	2	9	1	3	5	6	8	4
1	3	4	8	2	6	79	59	579
9	8	2	4	1	3	5	7	6
5	46	1	67	8	27	24	39	39
3	46	7	569	59	29	24	1	8

The 79-79 twin pair in the first row clears out the 9's from the other cells, giving another twin pair 35-35 in the first row. Except for the fourth cell in the last row, and the last cell in the sixth row, all of the empty cells now contain only two possibilities. This is the kind of situation where XY-wings tend to be present. And indeed we discover one here, in the three circled cells (next page).

8	1	6	35 / 4	(79)	79 / 35 / 2

The grid:

8	1	6	³⁵4	⑦⑨	⁷⁹ ³⁵ 2
4	9	3	2	㊹⑦ 1	8 6 ⁵⁷
2	7	5	³⁹6	8	1 4 ³⁹
6	5	8	⁷⁹ ⁷⁹ 4	3	2 1
7	2	9	1 3 5	6	8 4
1	3	4	8 2 6	⁷⁹	⁵⁹ ⁵⁷⁹
9	8	2	4 1 3	5	7 6
5	⁴⁶1	⁶⁷8	²⁷	²⁴ ³⁹ ³⁹
3	⁴⁶7	⁵⁶⁹ ㊹⑨ ²⁹2	²⁴	1 8

The cell containing 57 is the pivot of the XY-wing. If the value there is 5, then the lowest cell of the XY-wing contains the 9. If the value in the pivot cell is 7, then the upper cell of the XY-wing contains the 9. Either way, any cell which 'sees' both the lower and the upper cell cannot contain 9 as a possibility. Here, the two cells which 'see' both cells of the XY-wing are the cells which belong to both the sixth column and square 8. Only the lowest cell of the sixth column contains 9 as a possibility. The XY-wing technique thus shows that this cell must contain a 2. As often happens when many cells contain just two possibilities, the effect of this single digit bounces all over the puzzle, completing it easily.

8	1	6	5	4	9	7	3	2
4	9	3	2	7	1	8	6	5
2	7	5	3	6	8	1	4	9
6	5	8	7	9	4	3	2	1
7	2	9	1	3	5	6	8	4
1	3	4	8	2	6	9	5	7
9	8	2	4	1	3	5	7	6
5	4	1	6	8	7	2	9	3
3	6	7	9	5	2	4	1	8

Rule 6. The X-wing rule. If a given digit can only be in cell a or cell b of row A and in cell a or cell b of row B, then that digit appears in either cell A or cell B of column a and in either cell A or cell B of column b, allowing other possibilities for that digit in those columns to be erased. The rule also holds with the words 'row' and 'columns' exchanged, of course.

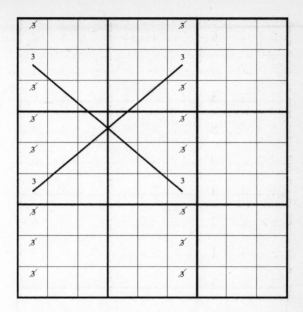

For instance, in this diagram, if we suppose that the first and sixth cells of row two and the first and sixth cells of row six are the only cells of those rows which can contain a 3, then the X-wing applies to those four possible 3's, eliminating all the other possible 3's from the first column and the sixth column.

Rule 6a. A generalisation of the X-wing rule (sometimes known as swordfish) is the same rule but with three cells instead of two: if a given digit can only appear in cells a, b and c of row A, cells a, b and c of row B and cells a, b and c of row C, then the possibility for that digit can be erased from all other cells of column a, column b and column c. It is important to note that this rule is still valid even if the digit does not actually appear in the possibilities of all nine cells. For instance, some of the nine cells can be already occupied by another digit, or some of them may contain other possibilities but not that precise digit. This makes no difference to the principle that all possibilities for that digit in the columns can be removed.

Rule 6b. The same rule obviously still holds for four or more cells, even though this is rarely useful in practice.

A sudoku using X-wing

	3			2	1			5
	1			8				
	9	8			3			4
9			3	5				
				6	4			8
2			7			6	1	
			9				7	
6			1	3			5	

This puzzle doesn't look too difficult to start with. The two 1's in the second column of squares yield a new 1 in square 5, the two 1's in the first row of squares yield the 1 in square 3, and the two 1's now in the third column of squares then yield the 1 in square 6.

	3			2	1			5
	1			8				
	9	8			3	1		4
9			3	5				1
				1				
				6	4			8
2			7			6	1	
				9			7	
6			1	3			5	

Now let us do some rapid scanning with the basic rules, in the places that already have several digits. The fifth column already contains seven digits, and the missing 7 and 4 can be placed, completing it. This makes squares 2, 5 and 8 look promising, but unfortunately none of their missing digits can be placed. Let us look at square 1, which has four digits. Here we are luckier, and find that the 2 can be placed, then the 6, and then the 5, leaving a 47-47 twin pair in this square. No such luck with square 9, which also contains four digits.

So let's now consider rows with several digits. We start with row three; the two missing digits are 2 and 6, and we can place the 6, then the 2. This gives two 6's in the second column of squares, and we can place the third one in square 8. Row seven has five digits, and the possibilities for the four empty cells are 58, 359, 58 and 39, which by the twin pair rule becomes two twin pairs. Row one has five digits, but its four empty cells contain the quadruple set of possibilities 47, 49, 789, 89.

Let us consider columns with many digits. The first column contains four digits and a twin pair, so the missing digits 1, 3 and 8 must live in the three empty cells outside of the twin pair; they form a triple. No other column has many digits, so let us place some pencil marks in the fullest areas and try to use some possibility-reducing techniques. We start with squares 2, 3, 5, 8 and 9.

47	3	6	49	2	1	789	89	5
47	1	2	459	8	59	379	369	367 9
5	9	8	6	7	3	1	2	4
9			3	5	278			1
38			289	1	278 9			
13			29	6	4			8
2	58	39	7	4	58	6	1	39
138			258	9	6	234 8	7	23
6			1	3	28	248 9	5	29

The three empty cells in square 2 form a triple, as do those in square 8. Square 5 contains a quadruple. However, the three cells with pencil marks 39, 23, 29 in square 9 form a triple, so by rule 3a, the remaining empty cells actually form a 48-48 twin pair. This in turn reduces the 789 pencil mark in the top cell of the eighth column to 79. Then we see that there is now only one cell in the first row which can contain the 8, so we place it. The remaining four empty cells in square 3 form a quadruple. Nothing more seems to happen, so let us fill in all the other pencil marks. Note that the triple at the bottom of the ninth column means that the two remaining empty cells in that column form a 67-67 twin pair.

An X-wing appears in rows four and seven, in each of which the 8 can only appear in the second and sixth cells.

47 3	6	49 2	1	79 8	5
47 1	2	459 8	59 379	369	367 9
5 9	8	6 7	3 1	2	4
9 246 78	147	3 5	278 247	46	1
38 245 678	345 7	289 1	278 9 234 579	346 9	236 79
13 257	135 7	29 6	4 235 79	39	8
2 58	39	7 4	58 6	1	39
138 458	134 5	258 9	6 48	7	23
6 247 8	479	1 3	28 48	5	29

Thus, rule 6 allows us to erase the 8 from the pencil marks in the other cells of the second and sixth columns, immediately yielding the 2 at the bottom of the sixth column. Apart from reducing the pencil marks in the ninth row and the sixth column, this now yields the 9 in square 9, then the 3 in square 9, then the 2 in square 9. Then the 9 in row seven appears, and erasing it from the pencil marks in the third column causes a 47-47 twin pair to appear in square 7.

47 · 3	6	49 · 2	1	79 · 8	5
47 · 1	2	459 · 8	59	379 · 369	67
5 · 9	8	6 · 7	3	1 · 2	4
9 · 246 78	147	3 · 5	78	247 · 46	1
38 · 245 67	345 7	289 · 1	79	234 579 · 346 9	67
13 · 257	135 7	29 · 6	4	235 79 · 39	8
2 · 58	9	7 · 4	58	6 · 1	3
138 · 45	134 5	58 · 9	6	48 · 7	2
6 · 47	47	1 · 3	2	48 · 5	9

Using the twin pair rule, we find the 5 in square 7, then the 8 in square 7. Then there is only one cell in row eight where the 4 can go, then only one where the 8 can go. Squares 8 and 9 are now complete. The 9 in the sixth column is now determined, then the 7, then the 8, completing this column. This causes a 29-29 twin pair to appear in the fourth column, determining the 4 at the top of that column by the twin pair rule. From this point on the puzzle is solved without any difficulty.

7	3	6	4	2	1	9	8	5
4	1	2	5	8	9	3	6	7
5	9	8	6	7	3	1	2	4
9	6	7	3	5	8	2	4	1
8	4	3	2	1	7	5	9	6
1	2	5	9	6	4	7	3	8
2	8	9	7	4	5	6	1	3
3	5	1	8	9	6	4	7	2
6	7	4	1	3	2	8	5	9

And finally...a difficult sudoku

	2		3				7	5
				6				4
9		1			2			
1		3					5	
	9		8		4		6	
	4					3		2
			4			5		3
5				7				
3	6				1		2	

Hint: after considering the digits 2, 3, 4, and using rule 3 in all its variants, look for an application of 6a.

...and an even more difficult sudoku

		5				4		
			3		9			
9	7		8		5		1	2
	9		1		3		4	
		3				5		
	6		2		4		8	
2	3		4		1		5	6
			6		7			
		7				1		

Hint: rule 5 again, and again, and again in all its shapes. Rule 4b comes in handy as well.

Chapter Two – Kakuro

A kakuru grid is made up of crossing 'blocks'. Each block is a line of boxes with a total number in a black box at its left or top end. Each block must be filled out with distinct digits adding up to the total number.

Easy Kakuro

In easy kakuro puzzles, the numbers are successively determined (usually starting from the corners) by short reasoning steps of the following type.

Zero-step (or automatic) entries

The automatic entries are those which are forced, either because they are in a block of length 1 or because they are the last missing number in an otherwise full block. In the left-hand example below, a 2 must be placed in the single box of

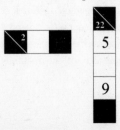

the 2-block. In the right-hand example, the total sum of the three boxes in the block must be 22 and a 5 and a 9 are already placed in two of the boxes, so the empty middle box must automatically contain an 8.

One-step entries

These are entries for which one can exclude all but one of the possible digits by consulting just one other box, or one other block. Here are three examples of different types, all of which occur frequently.

Exclusion of numbers already present in an intersecting block. In the left-hand example on page 73, the two boxes of the 3-block must contain a 2 and a 1, since this is the only way to decompose 3 into two boxes. Can the left-hand box contain the 2? Then the right-hand box contains the 1, but this is impossible since it would be in a vertical block already containing a 1. So the left-hand box of the 3-block must contain the 1, and the right-hand box the 2. In other words, *a digit cannot go into a block already containing the same digit.*

Exclusion of numbers which can't go into an intersecting block. In the middle example on page 73, the right-hand box of the horizontal 16-block must contain either a 7 or a 9, since 16 can only decompose into two boxes as 7 and 9. But if it contains the 9, then the vertical four-box 13-block contains a 9, so the remaining 13-9=4 must decompose into 3 boxes (4 must be a sum of three distinct digits), which is impossible. So the 7 goes in the right-hand box of the 16-block and the 9 in the left-hand box.

Unique intersection. The right-hand example below shows a configuration that arises very frequently in the corners of kakuro puzzles. The only way for 17 to decompose into two boxes is as an 8 and a 9. Can the left-hand box of the 17-block contain the 9? Then the right-hand box contains an 8, which would also be in the vertical 16-block, which would thus have to contain 8 and 8, impossible. Therefore the left-hand box of the 17-block must contain the 8, the right-hand box the 9, and the upper box of the 16-block must contain a 7. Another way of expressing this principle is: *if two blocks intersect and there is only one digit which occurs in both blocks, then that digit lies in the intersection box.* Typically, one often finds a two-box 3-block intersecting a two-box 4-block in the corner of kakuro puzzles. Since 3 can only decompose into two boxes as 1, 2 and 4 as 1, 3, the 1 necessarily goes in the intersecting box. Similarly, 16 can only decompose into two boxes 9, 7 and 17 can only decompose into two boxes as 9, 8, so if a two-box 16-block intersects a two-box 17-block, the 9 goes into the intersection box.

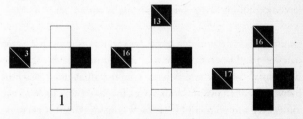

Another way of making the same reasoning is as follows: the two boxes of the 17-block must contain an 8 and a 9 (the only possible decomposition of 17 as the sum of two digits). The two boxes of the 16-block must contain a 7 and a 9 (the only possible decomposition of 16 as the sum of two digits). These two blocks intersect in one box, so that box must contain the 9, the only number common to the two decompositions.

Two-step entries

Crossing blocks. The left-hand box of the horizontal two-box 5-block in the diagram below can contain the digits 1, 2, 3 or 4.

If it contains 1, then the vertical 20-block of three boxes contains a 1, which means that 19 has to then decompose as a sum of two digits, which is impossible. If it contains 2, then the remaining 20-2=18 has to decompose as 2 different digits, again impossible. So it must contain a 3 or a 4.

We have come this far using only one-step reasoning, but now we need to decide between the 3 and the 4. The two-step reasoning to exclude the 3 is as follows. If the left-hand box of the 5-block contains a 3, then 20-3=17, so the upper two boxes in the vertical 20-block must contain an 8 and a 9 (reference to the 22-block). But both of these digits are too big to land in the horizontal three-box 10-block (reference to the horizontal 8-block). Therefore this configuration cannot occur, so the left-hand digit of the 5-block must be the 4, leading to filling out several other digits with ease.

Parallel blocks. Another typical two-step reasoning uses two parallel neighbouring blocks of the same length, like the horizontal 5-block and 6-blocks in the right-hand diagram below. The digits in the four boxes in these two blocks must altogether add up to 5+6=11. Now consider the vertical two-box 8-block and the vertical three-box 6-block. Together, those five digits must add up to 6+8=14. But four of the digits are the same as those in the horizontal 5-block and 6-block, and we already know those four add up to 11, so the remaining digit, the top digit in the vertical 6-block, must be 14-11=3.

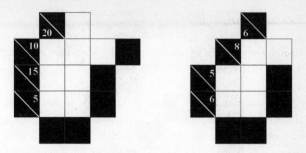

Easy kakuro puzzles are those in which numbers can be filled in successively with just the automatic or one-step or two-step type of reasoning explained above.

A very easy kakuro puzzle

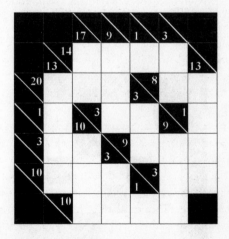

First place the four automatic 1's which go in blocks of length one.

Then the four 3-blocks which touch the edge of the puzzle can be filled out, since for each of them, the position of the 1 is determined by the fact that it can't go into a block already containing one of the 1's filled out previously.

There is now a two-box 8-block with a 1 in its left-hand box, so there is automatically a 7 in the right-hand box. This 7 lands in a vertical four-box 13-block which now already contains 7, 1 and 2, totalling 10, so the remaining empty box in the 13-block automatically contains a 3.

Now consider the two intersecting 3-blocks in the centre of the puzzle. Their intersection box can only contain a 1 or a 2. Suppose it is a 1. Then the box directly below it contains a 2, which lies in the horizontal three-box 9-block that now contains a 2 and a 3. This means that the middle box of the 9-block would contain a 4. But this 4 would lie in a vertical three-box 9-block already containing a 1, so that the remaining box would also have to contain a 4, which is impossible. We have shown that the intersection box of the 3-blocks must contain a 2. Eight other digits follow automatically.

Now consider the horizontal 14-block at the top of the puzzle, which already contains a 1 and a 2. Its first box intersects a vertical two-box 17-block, so it must contain either an 8 or a 9. If it contains a 9, the horizontal 14-block becomes 9, 2, 1, 2, which is impossible. So it contains an 8. The remaining digits appear automatically. The puzzle is done.

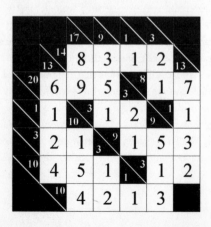

An easy kakuro puzzle

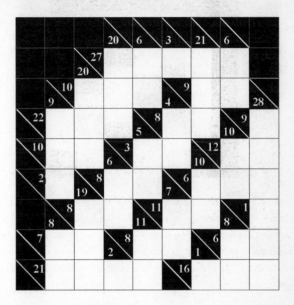

Six digits can be filled into the grid automatically because they belong to blocks with only one box.

Now we look for one-step entries. In the middle of the puzzle, in the fourth and fifth lines of the grid, we perceive an intersection of a two-box 3-block with a two-box 4-block. Remember that since 3 must be a 1 and a 2 and 4 has to be a 1 and a 3, only the digit 1 can be placed in the intersection box. Seven additional digits now appear automatically.

Now consider the vertical three-box 21-block at the top of the seventh column of the grid. Its third box contains a 5, so the top two boxes must add up to 16. Therefore they can only contain a 9 and a 7. The 9 cannot go in the middle box, because it would also lie in a horizontal 9-block. So the 7 goes in the middle box, and the 9 in the top box. Two more digits then appear automatically.

Now let us turn to the lower right-hand corner of the puzzle. There is a horizontal three-box 16-block at the bottom, whose first box already contains a 1. So the next two boxes must sum to 15, so they contain 6, 9 or 7, 8 or 8, 7 or 9, 6. The 6, 9 possibility is excluded because the 9 would appear in a vertical 28-block that already contains a 9. The 8, 7 and 9, 6 possibilities are excluded because the first digit (8 or 9) is too big to also appear in the vertical 8-block that intersects the 16-block. So the 16-block is 1, 7, 8. Two more digits appear automatically.

Look at the vertical 28-block on the right of the puzzle. It contains 9, 1, 5 and 8 which sum to 23, so the remaining 2 boxes must sum to 5. The lower of the two also lies in a three-box 6-block. Now, 6 can only decompose into three boxes as 1, 2 and 3, so the lower of the two empty boxes in the 28-block can only contain a 1, a 2 or a 3. It can't contain a 1 since a 1 already appears in the 28-block. If it contains a 3, then the upper empty box in the 28-block contains a 2. But this box also lies in a two-box 12-block, so the other box would have to contain 10, which is impossible. Therefore the upper empty box in the 28-block contains 3 and the lower one contains 2. Filling them in gives rise to eight further automatic digits.

Let us fill up the lower left-hand corner. The horizontal 21-block at the bottom already contains 2 and 6, so the first two boxes must add up to 13. They can be 4, 9 or 5, 8 or 6, 7 or 7, 6 or 8, 5 or 9, 4. But the 21-block already contains a 6, so we are reduced to four possibilities. The first digit cannot be an 8 or a 9 because this digit lies in a box which also belongs to a vertical 8-block, so we are reduced to 4, 9 or 5, 8. But the first digit cannot be a 4 since it lies in a vertical 8-block which would have to contain 4, 4. So the boxes contain 5, 8, and two further digits appear automatically.

Now consider the second box in the fourth row of the grid. It lies in the intersection of a vertical three-box 9-block and a horizontal three-box 22 block. This box cannot contain 1, 2, 3 or 4, because 22−1=21, 22−2=20, 22−3=19 and 22−4=18, and none of these four numbers can decompose into a sum of two different digits. The box cannot contain 7, 8 or 9 because the vertical 9-block already contains a 2, making those digits too big. The box can also not contain a 5, otherwise the 9-block would have to contain 5, 2, 2. So it contains a 6. Two more digits appear automatically.

Now the horizontal three-box 22-block contains a 6, so the remaining two boxes must add up to 16, so they can only contain a 9 and a 7. The 9 cannot go above the other 9 (in the vertical 20-block), so the 22-block decomposes as 6, 7, 9. A 4 automatically appears in the vertical 20-block above the 7.

Kakuro grid:

		20\	6\	3\	21\	6\		
	\27 20\			**3**	**9**	**4**		
\10 9\	**4**			\9 4\	**7**	**2**	28\	
22\	**6**	**7**	**9**	\8 5\	**3**	**5**	\9 10\	**9**
10\	**1**	**9**	\3 6\	**2**	**1**	\12 10\	**9**	**3**
2\	**2**	\8 19\	**5**	**3**	\6 7\	**3**	**1**	**2**
\8 8\	**7**	**1**	\11 11\	**4**	**7**	\1 8\	**1**	
7\	**3**	**4**	\8 2\	**5**	**3**	\6 1\	**1**	**5**
21\	**5**	**8**	**2**	**6**	\16	**1**	**7**	**8**

To finish, we consider the vertical three-box 20-block which already contains a 9. The remaining two boxes must add up to 11. The possibility 2, 9 (with 2 in the top box) is excluded because there is already a 9 in the 20-block. The possibilities 3, 8 and 4, 7 are excluded because 3 and 4 already occur in the horizontal 27-block. The possibility 5, 6 is excluded because the 6 also lies in a horizontal three-box 10-block that already contains a 4. The possibility 6, 5 remains. The possibility 7, 4 is excluded because the 4 also lies in the 10-block that already contains a 4. The possibility 8, 3 is excluded because if the 10-block contains 4 and 3, it must contain another 3. The possibility 9, 2 is excluded because the 27-block already contains a 9. So the only possibility is 6, 5 and the remaining digits appear automatically.

And finally...a very easy kakuro for the reader

Medium Kakuro

In this section we introduce a further technique for solving kakuro which makes its appearance heavily in all but the easiest puzzles. It uses the following table.

Number	Number of boxes	Digits
3	2	1, 2
4	2	1, 3
16	2	7, 9
17	2	8, 9
6	3	1, 2, 3
7	3	1, 2, 4
23	3	6, 8, 9
24	3	7, 8, 9
10	4	1, 2, 3, 4
11	4	1, 2, 3, 5
29	4	5, 7, 8, 9
30	4	6, 7, 8, 9
15	5	1, 2, 3, 4, 5
16	5	1, 2, 3, 4, 6
34	5	4, 6, 7, 8, 9
35	5	5, 6, 7, 8, 9
21	6	1, 2, 3, 4, 5, 6
22	6	1, 2, 3, 4, 5, 7
38	6	3, 5, 6, 7, 8, 9
39	6	4, 5, 6, 7, 8, 9
28	7	1, 2, 3, 4, 5, 6, 7
29	7	1, 2, 3, 4, 5, 6, 8
41	7	2, 4, 5, 6, 7, 8, 9
42	7	3, 4, 5, 6, 7, 8, 9
36	8	1, 2, 3, 4, 5, 6, 7, 8

Number	Number of boxes	Digits
37	8	1, 2, 3, 4, 5, 6, 7, 9
38	8	1, 2, 3, 4, 5, 6, 8, 9
39	8	1, 2, 3, 4, 5, 7, 8, 9
40	8	1, 2, 3, 4, 6, 7, 8, 9
41	8	1, 2, 3, 5, 6, 7, 8, 9
42	8	1, 2, 4, 5, 6, 7, 8, 9
43	8	1, 3, 4, 5, 6, 7, 8, 9
44	8	2, 3, 4, 5, 6, 7, 8, 9

Unique decomposition. What the table shows is that certain numbers – those in the left-hand column – can only decompose into three, four, five, six, seven, eight or nine boxes in a unique way. In the table, the number in the left-hand column decomposes into a number of boxes shown in the middle column, which must necessarily contain the digits in the last column. This technique applies whenever one of these decompositions occurs in the kakuro, and it serves to eliminate some possible digits from that block. For instance if a seven-box 41-block occurs, we know that the digits 2, 4, 5, 6, 7, 8 and 9 appear in the block, and 1 and 3 do not appear.

A medium kakuro puzzle

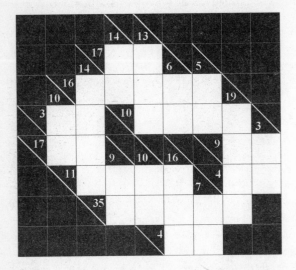

This puzzle contains several numbers from the table. For instance, it contains a four-box 10-block, which decomposes uniquely into 1, 2, 3, 4, and a four-box 11-block, which decomposes uniquely into 1, 2, 3, 5. It contains a five-box 16-block, which decomposes uniquely into 1, 2, 3, 4, 6, and a five-box 35-block, which decomposes uniquely into 5, 6, 7, 8, 9.

The first thing to fill out in this kakuro is the last box in the sixth row of the grid, which lies in the intersection of a two-box 3-block with a two-box 4-block. As we have already seen, only a 1 can lie in this box, giving three digits in the puzzle. Now we can apply our first example of the *unique decomposition* technique. Consider the 4-block in the last row of the puzzle. It must decompose as 1, 3 or 3, 1. If it decomposes as 1, 3, then the 3 also lies in a vertical 7-block whose top digit is thus 4. But we know from the table that a 4 cannot occur in the horizontal five-box 35-block! So the 4 decomposes as 3, 1 and the 7-block contains 6 as its top digit.

Now consider the vertical three-box 16-block at the bottom of the sixth column of the grid. It contains a 3 in the lowest box, so the upper two boxes add up to 13. Therefore they can contain 4, 9 or 5, 8 or 6, 7 or 7, 6 or 8, 5 or 9, 4 (in the order top box, middle box). Now we again invoke the unique decomposition principle. The top box lies in a horizontal four-box 11-block which by the table must contain 1, 2, 3, 5. Therefore the only legitimate possibility in the above list is 5, 8.

Now consider the vertical two-box 9-block at the bottom of the fourth column of the grid. Since the top box lies in the 11-block, it can only contain 1, 2 or 3. Therefore the 9-block must decompose as 1, 8 or 2, 7 or 3, 6. But both 8 and 6 already appear in the 35-block, so only 2, 7 remains.

Again by unique decomposition, we know that the 35-block contains 5, 6, 7, 8 and 9. The 6, 7 and 8 are already present, only the 5 and the 9 are missing. Note that the 9 cannot appear in the rightmost box of the 35-block, because this box also belongs to a vertical four-box 19-block which already contains 7 and 3. So the 5 must go in that box, producing four further automatic digits.

Now look at the 17-block at the beginning of the fifth row of the grid. We know it contains an 8 and a 9. If the second digit is a 9, then this 9 also belongs to a vertical four-box 14-block which already contains a 3. So 14-9-3=2 must decompose into two boxes, which is impossible. So the first box of the 17-block contains the 9 and the second box the 8. Three further digits appear automatically above these.

This brings us naturally to the horizontal five-box 16-block in the third row of the grid, which now contains a 1 as its first digit. We now by the unique decomposition table that the other boxes contain 2, 3, 4, 6. The second box of the 16-block belongs to a vertical two-box 14-block, and 2, 3 and 4 are too small to be there, so the second box must contain the 6. Two more automatic digits are produced above. Now the vertical three-box 13-block contains a 9 as its top digit, so the other two boxes must contain 1 and 3. The middle box cannot contain the 1 since there is already a 1 in that row.

Finally, the vertical 6-block must have a 2 or a 4 as its top digit since 16 decomposes as 1, 2, 3, 4, 6 and 1, 3, 6 are already present in the 16-block. But the lower digit can't be a 4, since that already appears in the 10-block, so the lower digit is a 2 and the upper digit is a 4. The last two digits appear automatically. The puzzle is finished.

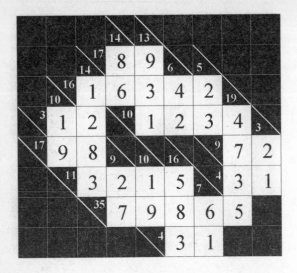

And finally...a couple of medium kakuros

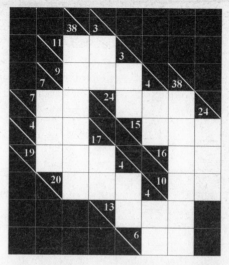

Really easy...if you know how to decompose 38 as a sum of 6 digits

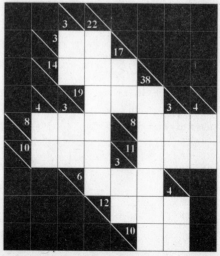

Difficult Kakuro

Let us introduce two last techniques for solving the most difficult kakuro puzzles. Both of them are extremely reminiscent of the techniques in sudoku. The difficult kakuro puzzles presented here were constructed by computer and can be found on the seemingly infinitely fertile website of Vegard Hannsen at:

http://www.menneske.no/kakuro/eng

These puzzles are reproduced here with his permission, which the author gratefully acknowledges. The site also contains a gigantic number of computer-generated sudoku.

Unique placement. If we know that a certain digit must appear in a given block, for example because of unique decomposition, we can test a given digit in every box in the block; sometimes, by elimination, we can find the unique box into which that digit can go.

A difficult kakuro puzzle

The solution of the following difficult puzzle uses a combination of the techniques *unique intersection*, *unique decomposition* and *unique placement*:

To begin with, there are a few entries that can be filled out automatically in this grid. There can't be a 9 in the upper left corner, otherwise the 11-block would contain 9, 1, 1. So there is a 7 there and a 9 just below it. The vertical 16-block in the upper-right corner must contain a 9 in its upper box and a 7 in its lower box, since it now cannot have a 9 in its lower box.

There cannot be a 1 in the last box of the fourth row, since a two-box 11-block cannot contain a 1. This then means that the vertical 3-block in the second column of the puzzle must contain a 2 in its upper box (in the same line as the 1), and a 1 in its lower box. These numbers and those that follow automatically are shown in the grid below.

Now let us invoke intersection and unique decomposition to place some isolated numbers.

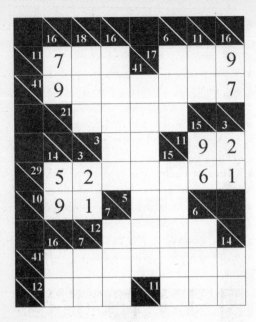

Consider the intersection of the seven-box 41-block in the eighth row of the puzzle and the vertical three-box 6-block at the bottom of the sixth column of the puzzle. The table shows that 6 can only decompose into three boxes as 1, 2, 3, whereas 41 can only decompose into seven boxes as 2, 4, 5, 6, 7, 8, 9. The only number that appears in both is 2, so the 2 is placed at the intersection. The identical reasoning places a 2 in the intersection of the horizontal 41-block in the second row of the puzzle and the vertical 6-block in the fifth column.

Now consider the same 41-block and the vertical three-box 7-block at the bottom of the third column of the puzzle. The table shows that 7 can only decompose into three boxes as 1, 2, 4. Both the 2 and the 4 also occur in the decomposition of 41 as 2, 4, 5, 6, 7, 8, 9, but the 2 already appears elsewhere in the 41-block, so the number to be placed at the intersection of the 41-block and the 7-block is 4.

Now we note that the vertical 41-block in the fourth column of the puzzle intersects the two-box 3-block in the fourth row, and since the decomposition of 41 into seven boxes cannot contain a 1, the intersection box must contain a 2 and the other box of the 3-block a 1. Since the horizontal 11-block in the upper left-hand corner of the puzzle contains a 7, the remaining two boxes add up to 11-7=4, so they contain a 1 and a 3. The new 1 automatically shows that the 11-block is 7, 1, 3 in that order. Then the 1 in the middle box of the 11-block also occurs in the upper box of a vertical three-box 18-block, whose two lower boxes thus contain 9 and 8. The middle box can't contain 9 since it is in a block which already does, so it contains 7 and the lower box 8.

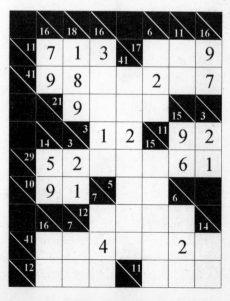

Note now that 29 decomposes uniquely into seven boxes as 1, 2, 3, 4, 5, 6, 8, and consider its intersection with the vertical 41-block in the fourth column of the puzzle. Since the 1, 2, 5 and 6 of the 29-block are already placed, and 3 does not occur in the decomposition of 41 into seven boxes, the intersection must be either 4 or 8. If it were 4, the 8 would go to the left or right of it. On the left, it would lie in a vertical five-box 16-block, so 16-8=8 would have to decompose into four boxes – impossible. On the right, it would belong to a vertical five-box 15-block, so 15-8=7 would have to decompose into four boxes, even more impossible. Therefore the 8 belongs in the intersection box of the vertical 41-block and the horizontal 29-block. It will have the 3 and the 4 on either side of it. Since the 3 cannot belong to the vertical 16-block which already contains a 3, the 4 goes to the left and the 3 to the right.

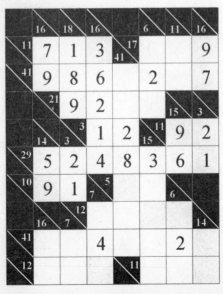

Now consider the vertical five-box 16-block; it already contains 1, 3 and 4, so the remaining 8 splits into two boxes. They can't contain 1 and 7 (the 1 is already in the block) or 3 and 5 (the 3 is already in the block) so they contain 2 and 6. The 2 cannot be in the upper empty box since there is already a 2 in that row, so the 6 is there, and the 2 lies in the third box of the 16-block.

Only a 4 and a 5 are missing from the 41-block in the second row. We can locate them by unique placement. If the 5 went into the second empty box, it would be in a vertical 11-block, so the upper box would contain 6, and the box to the left of that would necessarily contain 2, contradicting the 2 just below it. So that box contains 4 and the remaining empty box, in the vertical 41-block, contains 5. The whole upper half of the puzzle now fills up automatically.

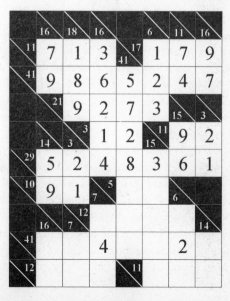

Consider now the two-box 5-block in the sixth row of the puzzle. It can decompose as 1, 4 or 2, 3 or 3, 2 or 4, 1, but the possibility 2, 3 is excluded because there is already a 2 in the vertical 41-block, and the possibilities 1, 4 and 3, 2 are excluded because the digits 1 and 3 cannot occur in the 41-block by the unique decomposition of 41 as seven boxes. So we place 4, 1 in the 5-block.

Only the digits 6 and 9 are missing from the vertical 41-block now. We use unique placement to determine the place for the 9. The 9 cannot go into the horizontal four-box 12-block, since the remaining 12−9=3 cannot decompose into 3 boxes. So the 6 goes there and the 9 just below it.

This shows that the vertical 16-block at the bottom of the first column of the puzzle must contain a 7 in its upper box and a 9 in its lower box.

	16	18	16		6	11	16
11\	7	1	3	17\41	1	7	9
41\	9	8	6	5	2	4	7
	21\	9	2	7	3	15\3	
14\3	3\		1	2	11\15	9	2
29\	5	2	4	8	3	6	1
10\	9	1	7\5	4	1	6\	
	16\7	12\7		6			14\
41\	7		4	9		2	
12\	9			11\			

Now the 41-block in the eighth row of the puzzle is almost full; there are three empty boxes which must contain the digits 5, 6 and 8. We can use unique placement to place the 8. It can't go in the first empty box, which intersects a vertical 7-block. It can't go in the second empty box, which belongs to a vertical five-block 15-box already containing a 1 and a 3, since the remaining total 15-8-1-3=3 would have to decompose as a 1 and a 2, repeating the 1 already in the 15-block. So the 8 must go in the last box of the 41-block, and an automatic 6 appears below it.

Now we place the 6 in the 41-block. It can't go in the vertical five-box 15-block either, because the total 15-6-1-3=5 would have to decompose either as 1+4 or 2+3, and both of these combinations repeat a number already in the block. So the 6 goes in the vertical 7-block and the 5 in the vertical

15-block. Several new digits appear automatically.

We can now easily finish the puzzle by considering the horizontal four-box 12-block in the seventh row of the puzzle, which contains the digits 1 and 6. The remaining two boxes must add up to 5, but they cannot contain 1 and 4 since there is already a 1 in the block. The leftmost box cannot contain 3 since there is a 3 in the vertical block, so it contains 2 and the rightmost box of the 12-block contains 3.

	16	18	16		6	11	16
11	7	1	3	17/41	1	7	9
41	9	8	6	5	2	4	7
	21	9	2	7	3	15	3
	14/3	3	1	2	11/15	9	2
29	5	2	4	8	3	6	1
10	9	1	7/5	4	1	6	
	16	12/7	1	6	2	3	14
41	7	6	4	9	5	2	8
12	9	1	2	11	4	1	6

And finally...a difficult kakuro

109

Very Difficult Kakuro

The last principle we introduce for solving kakuro is, like unique placement, very reminiscent of sudoku.

Twin pairs. This is a modification of the unique placement principle. If a given box in some block can only take two possible digits (say 1 or 3), and another box in the same block can also only take those two same possible digits, then one of them necessarily goes in one of the boxes and the other in the other, though we don't know which goes in which. But the two digits cannot appear in any other box of the block.

A very difficult kakuro puzzle

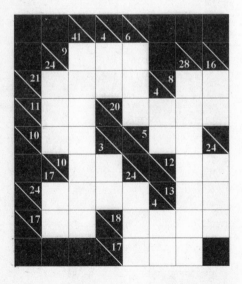

It's hard to find a place to get started on this puzzle. As usual, two-box blocks are the first place to look, and it is indeed easy to see that the vertical 16-block on the right of the puzzle must contain 7, 9, in that order from top to bottom, since the top digit belongs to a horizontal 8-block. But there are no other such simple observations.

Consider, however, the horizontal two-box 10-block in the fifth line of the grid. The left-hand digit of this block belongs to a vertical three-box 24-block, and thus the digits 1, 2, 3, 4, 5 and 6 are all too small to be on the left (since none of the numbers $24-1=23$, $24-2=22$, $24-3=21$, $24-4=20$, $24-5=19$ and $24-6=18$ can decompose as a sum of two distinct digits). So the 10-block must decompose as 7, 3 or 8, 2 or 9, 1. Now, the right-hand digit lies in the vertical seven-box 41-block, which by unique decomposition contains the digits 2, 4, 5, 6,

7, 8, 9, and cannot contain 1 or 3. This leaves only the possibility 8, 2 for the 10-block.

The same reasoning on the 24-block shows that the two-box 11-block just above the 10-block can only decompose as 7, 4 or 8, 3 or 9, 2. But the same reasoning on the 41-block shows that 3 cannot appear, so the 11-block must contain 7, 4. The 9 appears automatically in the 24-block.

Now let us test unique placement for the remaining digits in the 41-block, which by the unique decomposition table are 5, 6, 7, 8, 9.

* The 7, the 8 and the 9 cannot go into the top box since they are too big to belong to the horizontal 9-block. So the top box must contain 5 or 6.

* The second box can only contain 7 or 8, since the remaining numbers can total to as little as 3 or as much as 5 (but if they totalled to 3, the second box would contain 9 which already belongs to the horizontal block).

* The third box of the 41-block contains 4.

* The fourth box of the 41-block contains 2.

* The fifth box belongs to a horizontal 10-block which can only decompose as 8, 2 or 9, 1 since the second digit belongs to a 3-block. So the fifth box can only contain 8 or 9.

* The sixth box can contain 5, 6, 7, 8 or 9.

* The seventh box can only contain 8 or 9 since it belongs to a horizontal two-box 17-block.

From this list, we see that the fifth and seventh boxes form a twin pair for the digits 8 and 9, which thus cannot appear in the rest of the block. In particular, they cannot appear in the second box, so the second box must contain the 7.

This means that the horizontal four-box 21-block in the third line of the grid now begins 9, 7, and the remaining two digits must add up to 5. The first digit can only be 1 or 3, and the second can only be 1, 2 or 3, so the only possibility to add up to 5 is 3, 2. Placing these automatically fills up the top horizontal 9-block, showing that the top box of the 41-block contains 5. Now 2, 4, 5 and 7 are placed in the 41-block and the fifth and seventh boxes are twins for 8 and 9, so the 6 must go in the sixth box.

A very simple reasoning now completes the horizontal four-box 20-block in the fourth line of the grid. It starts with a 1 and ends with a 9, so the intervening two digits sum to 10, and the leftmost one belongs to a 4-block so it is either 1 or 3. But it can't be 1 since there is already a 1 in the block, so it is 3 and the third digit is 7. The 5-block below the 20-block is then automatically filled with 1, 4. The top half of the grid is filled.

We can now fill the horizontal four-box 24-block in the seventh row of the grid by a simple three-step reasoning. The second box contains 6, and the first can contain either 8 or 9 since it belongs to a vertical 17-block. Suppose the first contains an 8. Then the box just below it contains 9, the box to the right of that (the lowest box of the 41-block) contains 8 and the only empty box of the 41-block, the fifth box, contains 9. This box belongs to a horizontal 10-block which then decomposes as 9, 1. The 1 belongs to a vertical 3-block which then decomposes as 1, 2, with the 2 appearing as the third digit in our horizontal four-box 24-block. So the 24-block decomposes as 8, 6, 2, *, (where the star represents a number that has not yet been determined) and the final digit must be...an 8, which is impossible.

Therefore the first digit of the 24-block is a 9, allowing us to automatically fill out several digits.

Now consider the vertical three-box 24-block at the bottom of the fifth column of the grid. It starts with an 8, so the remaining two digits must sum to 16, so they are 7 and 9. Suppose the 7 is the lowest digit. It lies in a horizontal three-box 17-block, whose second digit can only be 1 or 3. So the 17-block could decompose as 7, 1, 9 or 7, 3, 7. The second scenario is obviously impossible. But the first (7, 1, 9) is impossible by unique decomposition, since the 9 would have to belong to a vertical seven-box 28-block, which by the unique decomposition table must contain the digits 1, 2, 3, 4, 5, 6, 7 and neither 8 nor 9.

Therefore the vertical 24-block decomposes from top to bottom as 8, 7, 9 and the horizontal 17-block as 9, 1, 7 or 9, 3, 5. The first possibility is eliminated by the fact that the 7 would lie in the vertical 28-block which already contains a 7. So the 17-block decomposes as 9, 3, 5.

The missing digits in the vertical 28-block are 2, 3 and 6. Consider the horizontal two-box 12-block that intersects the 28-block. Its left-hand box can't contain either a 2 or a 6, so it must contain the 3, and the right-hand box a 9. Just below this 12-block is a two-box 13-block intersecting the 28-block, which also can't contain a 2, so it must contain the 6, and its other digit is 7. The 2 goes in the last empty box of the 28-block and the final 8 is automatic. The puzzle is finished.

An extremely difficult kakuro puzzle

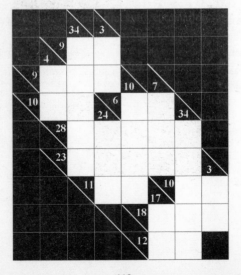

Again, the hardest part is finding a place to start. The two-box blocks are as usual the most promising. Now consider the horizontal 9-block at the top left of the puzzle. It can contain 7, 2 or 8, 1 since its second digit lies in a 3-block. If it contains 7, 2, then the horizontal three-box 9-block just below it contains a 1 as its third digit. So it can be 6, 2, 1 or 5, 3, 1 or 3, 5, 1 or 2, 6, 1. But the leftmost digit also belongs to a vertical 4-block so only the possibility 3, 5, 1 remains. But the middle digit has to belong to the vertical five-box 34-block, which by the table decomposes as 4, 6, 7, 8, 9. This doesn't contain a 5, so our assumption that the top 9-block decomposes as 7, 2 is wrong. It must decompose as 8, 1.

Now look at the horizontal two-box 12-block at the very bottom of the puzzle can contain 8, 4 or 9, 3 (since the left-hand box belongs to a vertical 17-block. But the 9, 3 possibility is excluded since the second box belongs to a five-box 34-block which according to the table decomposes uniquely as 4, 6, 7, 8, 9. The decomposition doesn't contain a 3, so the 12-block must contain 8, 4. This means that the first box of the horizontal 18-block just above the 12-block must contain a 9, so since the last digit is 1 or 2 (belonging to a 3-block), we have either 9, 8, 1 or 9, 7, 2 for the 18-block.

If the 18-block contains 9, 8, 1 then the box just above the 1 automatically contains a 2, and the box to the left of that must then contain an 8, which is just over the other 8! This is impossible, so the 18-block contains 9, 7, 2, and two more digits appear automatically.

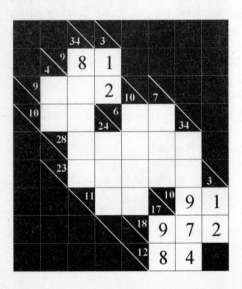

Let us now consider the horizontal 23-block. Its last digit has to be either 6 or 8 since it belongs to the vertical 34-block that decomposes as 4, 6, 7, 8, 9. Suppose it is 6. Then 23-6=17 decomposes into four boxes, of which the leftmost one also belongs to a five-box 34-block, so is equal to 4, 6, 7 or 9.

If 23=9, *, *, *, 6 then 23-9-6=8. The number 8 decomposes into three boxes as 1, 2, 5 or 1, 3, 4, but all of the digits 1, 2, 3, 4 or 5 are too small to go into the vertical three-box 24-block that intersects the second box of the 23-block.

If 23=7, *, *, *, 6 then 23-7-6=10 and this 10 must decompose into three boxes as 1, 2, 7 or 1, 3, 6 or 1, 4, 5 or 2, 3, 5. The first two possibilities are excluded since 6 and 7 already occur in the 23-block, and the second two possibilities only contain the digits 1, 2, 3, 4, 5 which we already saw are too small to go in the vertical 24-block.

Obviously we can't have 23=6, *, *, *, 6. Let's test 23=4, *, *, *, 6. Here we have to break up 23-4-6=13 into the three middle boxes of the 23-block. We can break up 13 as 1, 3, 9 or 1, 4, 8 or 1, 5, 7 or 2, 3, 8 or 2, 4, 7 or 2, 5, 6 or 3, 4, 6, but all of the possibilities containing either 4 or 6 are impossible, so we have to examine only 1, 3, 9, 1, 5, 7 and 2, 3, 8.

For the possibility 1, 3, 9, the 1 would have to go into the vertical three-box 7-block (which decomposes uniquely as 1, 2, 4) and the 3 into the vertical four-box 10-block, which decomposes uniquely as 1, 2, 3, 4. So the 9 would have to go into the vertical 24-block. But then this vertical box would have to contain 5, 9, 8 or 8, 9, 5 (from top to bottom). The 8, 9, 5 possibility would give a 6 next to the 5 in the horizontal 11-block. But this 6 would also lie in the vertical 10-block, which is impossible. The 5, 9, 8 possibility would give an 8 in the 11-block, so the other digit would be a 3, just under the 3 already present in the 10-block.

The possibility 1, 5, 7 is easier to exclude since only the 1 can be either in the vertical 7-block or the vertical 10-block.

The possibility 2, 3, 8 must have the 2 in the vertical 7-block and the 3 in the vertical 10-block, so the 8 goes in the vertical 24-block, which then must read 9, 8, 7 or 7, 8, 9 from top to bottom. If the 7 is at the bottom, the right-hand box of the 11-block contains 4, so the upper two boxes of the vertical 10-block contain 1 and 2, but either order for these two digits gives an immediate contradiction with the 7-block. If the 9 is at the bottom, then the right-hand box of the 11-block contains a 2, so the upper two boxes of the 10-block contain 1 and 4, but again either order gives an immediate contradiction with the 7-block.

We have excluded all possibility for the last digit of the 23-block to be 6, so we now know that it is 8 and the last digit of the 28-block is 6.

Now let's concentrate on the first box of the 23-block, which as we saw can contain 4, 6, 7 or 9. If it contains 6, 7 or 9, then the middle three boxes must add up to 9, 8 or 7, which decompose into three boxes as $9=1+2+6$ or $1+3+5$ or $2+3+4$, $8=1+2+5$ or $1+3+4$, $7=1+2+4$. But as we saw earlier, all the digits from 1 to 6 are too small to go in the vertical 24-block.

So the leftmost digit of the 23-block can only be 4. Now, the only two possibilities for the horizontal 9-block in the third row of the grid were 1, 6, 2 and 3, 4, 2 since the last digit 2 is already there and the first must belong to a 4-block. But the middle digit can't be a 4 since the 4 in the vertical 34-block is now placed, so the 9-block contains 1, 6, 2, yielding more automatic digits.

Let us continue trying to fill out the 23-block which now looks like 4, *, *, *, 8 where the three middle digits add up to 11. These three digits can thus be 1, 2, 8 or 1, 3, 7 or 1, 4, 6 or 2, 3, 6 or 2, 4, 5. We can throw out the first possibility because 8 already occurs in the 23-block and the last three possibilities because we already saw that all those digits are too small to go in the vertical 24-block. So the three middle digits are 1, 3, 7 and 1 must go in the 7-block, 3 in the 10-block and 7 in the 24-block.

Now the vertical 24-block can only read 9, 7, 8 or 8, 7, 9 from top to bottom, but the top digit is in the 28-block which already contains a 9, so the 24-block reads 8, 7, 9 from top to bottom, yielding enough automatic digits to finish the puzzle.

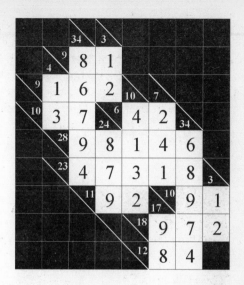

And to end with...quite a tough one!

Hint: start in the upper right-hand corner, then the lower right-hand corner

Appendix:
The Story of Magic Squares

Long, long before the phenomenal twenty-first century success of number-grid puzzles, the mysteries of magic squares fascinated mathematicians, magicians and laymen of all persuasions. The combinatorics and arithmetic of these deep and beautiful squares are what lie behind the sudoku and kakuro puzzles investigated in this book. The present appendix is for readers who may enjoy penetrating a little more deeply into the ideas behind magic-square type puzzles.

The original magic square puzzle consists in simply *creating* them. Can one finish putting the numbers 1 through 9 into the 3-by-3 grid in such a way that the sum of the numbers in every row, every column is equal to 15? Or the numbers 0 to

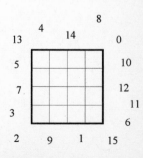

15 in the 4-by-4 grid to make all those row and column sums equal to 30?

Number arrangements possessing all kinds of mysterious and remarkable properties exist in a great variety of forms and sizes. The term 'magic' was coined because, seemingly miraculously, all of their rows and columns add up to the same total number. These squares have been the plaything of amateurs, philosophers and mathematicians for many centuries. Sudoku are, of course, magic squares, but unlike sudoku, the most-studied type of magic square, if it forms an n-by-n grid, contains exactly all the digits from 1 to n^2 (or from 0 to n^2-1).

Many of the deep questions concerning magic squares are currently unsolved problems: How many n-by-n magic squares are there? Is there some method to construct them all other than trial and error? How does one go about solving a given one? Yet the large amount of research they have generated over the centuries has given rise to all kinds of discoveries, amazing tricks, astute construction methods, and truly astounding squares capable of charming and intriguing people far outside the boundaries of the world of mathematics.

Magic, Diabolic, Panmagic and More...

Different Magic Squares

Magic squares can be more and more magic, gaining for each property a new and more impressive name. The basic magic square has rows, columns and the two main diagonals which all add up to the same number. That number, the magic number, depends only on the size of the square. If the square is an n-by-n grid, then the magic number is $n(n^2+1)/2$.

Magic squares whose rows and columns work but not the main diagonals are called *semi-magic*.

1	6	8
5	7	3
9	2	4

Diabolic squares (also sometimes called panmagic squares) have not only the two main diagonals adding up to the magic number, but also all the other diagonals obtained by starting anywhere and using 'wraparound'.

8	1	6
3	5	7
4	9	2

4	14	15	1
9	7	6	12
5	11	10	8
16	2	3	13

Bimagic squares are magic squares such that if you square every single entry, you obtain another magic square! It sounds impossible, yet they exist. The first one was discovered by a most intriguing figure: a certain mysterious G. Pfeffermann, who published his findings in the form of puzzles to be completed by the reader, in the January 1891 issue of *Les*

Tablettes du Chercheur, a nineteenth-century French journal of mathematical games and puzzles. We give the square below for the reader's appreciation – Pfeffermann left every other square blank, and published the full solution only two weeks later!

56	34	8	57	18	47	9	31
33	20	54	48	7	29	59	10
26	43	13	23	64	38	4	49
19	5	35	30	53	12	46	60
15	25	63	2	41	24	50	40
6	55	17	11	36	58	32	45
61	16	42	52	27	1	39	22
44	62	28	37	14	51	21	3

More than a century went by before the first trimagic square was finally discovered, by Walter Trump in 2002. This is a magic square such that if you cube every entry, you get another magic square!

1	22	33	41	62	66	79	83	104	112	123	144
9	119	45	115	107	93	52	38	30	100	26	136
75	141	35	48	57	14	131	88	97	110	4	70
74	8	106	49	12	43	102	133	96	39	137	71
140	101	124	42	60	37	108	85	103	21	44	5
122	76	142	86	67	126	19	78	59	3	69	23
55	27	95	135	130	89	56	15	10	50	118	90
132	117	68	91	11	99	46	134	54	77	28	13
73	64	2	121	109	32	113	36	24	143	81	72
58	98	84	116	138	16	129	7	29	61	47	87
80	34	105	6	92	127	18	53	139	40	111	65
51	63	31	20	25	128	17	120	125	114	82	94

One can go on and on – and people have – creating new variants on these magic squares, with different kinds of remarkable properties: the sums of 2-by-2 subsquares are all equal, the sums of diametrically opposed pairs of entries are equal, etc. etc. We are not going to delve into all of them here, although some very special ones are shown in the next section. Let us just end this little review with what seems to be the most astonishing discovery of all: the *addition-multiplication* magic square. This square is not only magic, but if you take the product of all the numbers in each row and each column, you also get the same total every time! Such a square is impossible using the numbers 1 to n^2; it is amazing that one can construct them at all. They were discovered by W. W. Horner in the 1950s.

162	207	51	26	133	120	116	25
105	152	100	29	138	243	39	34
92	27	91	136	45	38	150	261
57	30	174	225	108	23	119	104
58	75	171	90	17	52	216	161
13	68	184	189	50	87	135	114
200	203	15	76	117	102	46	81
153	78	54	69	232	175	19	60

Magic Squares in History and Art

The Lo-Shu square

Chinese literature from 2800 BC, when the Lo-Shu magic square (scroll of the river Shu) was invented by Fuh-Hi, the founder of Chinese civilisation. The story of Lo-Shu is that there was a terrible flood of the river Shu. The people tried to appease the river god with sacrifices, but each time they did so, a turtle came out of the river, walked around the sacrifice, and went back into the water, indicating that the sacrifice was not satisfactory. This went on until a small child noticed a curious design on the turtle's shell – the first 3-by-3 magic square! On the basis of the magic square, the people were able to calculate the correct amount for the sacrifice, and the flood went down.

Rabbi Abraham ben Ezra

In Western science, some form of the magic square appears in Greek writings from a thousand years BC, but the whole subject then seems to have lain dormant, although it is mentioned by Theon of Smyrna in 130 AD. However, by the Middle Ages the magic square had become quite popular as a tool for all forms of magic: astrology, alchemy, and plain good luck. Arabian astrologers used it in drawing up horoscopes. In India, the first known 4-by-4 magic square with a constant of 84 was said to be useful to soothe a crying child. The 3-by-3 magic square is mentioned in Arab writings in the ninth or tenth centuries, where it was said to ease the pains of childbirth; the Arabs also discovered larger magic squares.

The first magic square appears explicitly in European literature in the writings of Rabbi Abraham ben Ezra (1092-1167), who came from Muslim Spain and later travelled throughout much of Europe, spreading knowledge of Arabian accomplishments in mathematics, themselves often building on Indian mathematics and symbols introduced somewhat earlier. Rabbi ben Ezra wrote extensively on such subjects as grammar, exegesis, philosophy, medicine, astronomy, astrology, permutations and combinations, the calendar, the astrolabe and biblical studies. His three treatises on numbers taught Europeans about writing numbers with the system we use now; the second one introduces the famous zero. He was fascinated by number arrangements in connection with the science of Gematria, the study of the secret meanings contained in Judaic sacred texts obtained by assigning numerical values to the letters of the Hebrew alphabet and connecting words with the same total number. This science is still practiced extensively today, including by university mathematicians.

Cornelius Agrippa

The German philosopher Henry Cornelius Agrippa von Nettesheim (1486–1535) was counsellor to the Emperor Charles the Fifth, and was a prolific writer of Renaissance esoterica. In his book *De Occulta Philosophia*, he constructed seven magic squares of orders 3, 4, 5, 6, 7, 8, 9, and associated them to the seven known 'planets' of the time: Saturn, Jupiter, Mars, Sun, Venus, Mercury, Moon, in that order. He wrote:

'It is affirmed by Magicians, that there are certain tables of numbers distributed to the seven planets, which they call the sacred tables of the planets, endowed with many, and very great virtues of the Heavens, inasmuch as they represent that divine order of Celestiall numbers, impressed upon Celestials by the ideals of the divine mind, by means of the soul of the world, and the sweet harmony of those Celestial rayes, signifying according to the proportion of effigies, supercelestiall Intelligencies, which can in no other way be expressed, than by the marks of numbers, and Characters. For material numbers, and Figures can do nothing in the mysteries of hid things, but representatively by formall numbers, and figures, as they are governed and informed by intelligencies, and divine numerations, which unite the extreams of the matter, and spirit to the will of the elevated soul, receiving through great affection, by the Celestiall power of the operator, a power from God, applyed through the soul of the universe, and observations of Celestiall constellations, to a matter fit for a form, the mediums being disposed by the skill, and industry of Magicians; But let us hasten to explain the tables severally.'

There follows an explanation of each magic square, astrological in nature. For instance, the magic square associated to Jupiter is described as follows:

'It consists of a square drawn into itself: it contains sixteen particular numbers, and in every line and diameter four, making thirty-four: the sum of all is one hundred and thirty-six. There are over it Divine names, with an Intelligency to what is good, with a spirit to what is bad, and out of it is drawn the character of Jupiter and the spirit thereof; if this is engraven on a plate of silver, with Jupiter being powerful and reigning in the Heavens, it conduces to gain riches and favour, love, peace and concord, and to appease enemies, and to confirm honours, dignities and counsels; and it dissolves enchantments if graven on coral.'

4	14	15	1
9	7	6	12
5	11	10	8
16	2	3	13

6	32	3	34	35	1
7	11	27	28	8	30
19	14	16	15	23	24
18	20	22	21	17	13
25	29	10	9	26	12
36	5	33	4	2	31

The left-hand magic square is the Jupiter square, whereas the right-hand one is that corresponding to the Sun, with the following description:

'The fourth table is of the Sun, and is made of a square of six, and contains thirty-six numbers, whereof six in every side, and Diameter, produce 111, and the sum of all is 666. Over this are of Divine names set such names as fill up the numbers with an Intelligency to what is good, with a spirit to what is bad, and out of the same numbers is drawn the seal, or Character of the Sun, and of the spirits thereof, such as we shall beneath ascribe to its table. This being engraven on a Golden plate with the Sun being fortunate, renders him that wears it to be renowned, amiable, acceptable, potent in all his works, and equals a man to Kings, and Princes, elevating him to high fortunes, inabling him to do whatsoever he pleaseth: but with an unfortunate Sun, it makes a Tyrant, and a man to be proud, ambitious, unsatisfiable and to have an ill ending.'

Napoleon, anyone?

Albrecht Dürer

Dürer (1471–1528) was a Renaissance painter from Nürnberg, now in Germany but called an Imperial Free City at the time. In 1494, already an accomplished artist, he travelled to Italy, where, without actually meeting any well-known mathematicians, he learned a great deal about recreational mathematics. This topic was to fascinate him all his life. After this visit, he delved into the study of mathematical proportion and ruler-and-compass constructions, which he used extensively in his woodcuts.

He returned to Italy again in 1505-1507, now a famous artist, and more convinced than ever that there were mathematical secrets hidden behind artistic beauty. On returning from this visit, he determined to write a book on mathematics and its applications to art. In 1514, the last year of his mother's life, he made the famous engraving *Melancolia* showing a sorrowful female figure surrounded by various symbolic props. The striking element here is the 4-by-4 magic square shown above the woman's head.

16	3	2	13
5	10	11	8
9	6	7	12
4	15	14	1

This square is closely related to Agrippa's Jupiter square; it has been turned upside down (the top row of Agrippa's square is the bottom row here), and furthermore the middle two columns have been interchanged, which doesn't change the magic of the square, and has the charming advantage of causing the engraving's date 1514 to appear in the bottom row. Jupiter's influence was considered to be an astrological antidote to the melancholia caused by the influence of Saturn, which is certainly at least one of the reasons for which Dürer included it in his engraving. At that time, there was no clear definition of what might constitute a scientific method, and magic and astrology were considered sciences and taken very seriously. The painting includes a large number of alchemical and astrological symbols. Yet mathematics remained his major scientific interest, and in fact in 1525 Dürer became the author of the first-ever mathematics book to be written in German, *Unterweisung der Messung mit dem Zirkel und Richtheit*, a treatise on the ruler-and-compass constructions that fascinated him.

Bernard Frénicle de Bessy

Bernard Frénicle de Bessy (1605–75) was a passionate amateur mathematician. He was not alone; at that time, many if not all of France's best mathematicians were amateurs, such as for example Pierre de Fermat, author of the famous problem known as 'Fermat's last theorem'. Fermat and Frénicle were contemporaries and corresponded regularly. In fact, Frénicle is remembered for having solved some problems sent to him by Fermat on the very day he received them: the first one was to find a cube n such that $n + S(n)$ is a square, where $S(n)$ is the number of divisors of n.

In 1693, Frénicle published *De quarrez ou tables magiques*, in which he displayed a number of remarkable magic squares. The main result of his work was the counting of all possible 4-by-4 magic squres: he proved that there are exactly 880 truly different squares (counting those obtained by rotating or symmetrically reflecting others as being identical). Nobody knows exactly how he counted them, but he may have done it by hand. It only takes an hour or so to show that there is only one 3-by-3 magic square, so the 4-by-4 case could be done with patience over a matter of days. In those times when computers were not available, scientists were not frightened of long calculations!

Benjamin Franklin

Benjamin Franklin toyed with magic squares in 1736–7 when he was employed as a clerk of the Pennsylvania Assembly, producing some squares with remarkable properties.

He put his work aside later, convinced that such pursuits were mere foolishness, but was led to take them out, and create a similar square of dimension 16-by-16, by a casual conversation he had with a friend called Mr Logan. As he writes in his autobiography:

'Being one day in the country at the house of our common friend, the late learned Mr Logan, he showed me a folio French book filled with magic squares, wrote, if I forget not, by one M. Frénicle, in which, he said, the author had discovered great ingenuity and dexterity in the management of numbers; and, though several other foreigners had distinguished themselves in the same way, he did not recollect that any one Englishman had done anything of the kind remarkable. I said it was perhaps the mark of the good sense of our English mathematicians that they would not spend their time in things that were merely "difficiles nugae", incapable of any useful application.'

As it transpired not more than a few minutes later, Franklin had engaged, as a youth, in exactly this type of useless occupation, which he had put aside, no doubt, with his short pants:

'I then confessed to him that in my younger days, having once some leisure which I still think I might have employed more usefully, I had amused myself in making these kind of magic squares...'

There follows one of the most remarkable magic squares known to history.

52	61	4	13	20	29	36	45
14	3	62	51	46	35	30	19
53	60	5	12	21	28	37	44
11	6	59	54	43	38	27	22
55	58	7	10	23	26	39	42
9	8	57	56	41	40	25	24
50	63	2	15	18	31	34	47
16	1	64	49	48	33	32	17

Apart from the usual properties of a magic square, whose row, column and diagonal sums are all equal to 260, every half-row and half-column of Franklin's square sums to 130, as do all of what he called the 'bent rows', the rows of 8 x's, 8 y's, 8 z's and 8 u's in the following diagram.

Even more amazingly, the bent rows still all add to 260 if one starts them at any position in the square and uses wraparound. He further noticed that the sum of the four corner numbers and the four centre numbers is 260, and the sum of the eight numbers nearest (but not in) the corners is also 260. And there are even more symmetries in this square, if one looks for them.

The best part of this story is the end. Mr Logan having shown Franklin a magic square of order 16 and remarked upon how difficult it must have been to produce, Franklin simply could not resist the challenge, and rushed home to produce his own 16-by-16 magic square that very same evening. A truly astonishing production which, although not having main diagonal sums equal to the required 2056, possesses the additional property that any 4-by-4 square inside the large square also had numbers adding up to 2056.

'This I sent to our friend the next morning, who, after some days, sent it back in a letter with these words: "I return to thee they astonishing or most stupendous piece of the magical square, in which—" but the compliment is too extravagant, and therefore, for his sake as well as my own, I ought not to repeat it. Nor is it necessary; for I make no question but you will readily allow this square of 16 to be the most magically magical of any magic square ever made by any magician.'

Leonhard Euler

In 1776, the very year in which Benjamin Franklin presumably ceased to refer to himself as 'an Englishman', Leonhard Euler (1707–83) submitted a paper redacted in Latin to the Proceedings of the St Petersburg Academy. Called *De quadratis magicis*, the paper explains an astonishing new method for the construction of magic squares. The best feature of the method is that when one has once seen the construction method, there is no need to prove that the resulting square is magic: it is obvious from the method itself. The worst feature is that the method proceeds by creating an enormous number of 'candidate squares' and then adding conditions to ensure that they are magic. It turns out to be quite easy to find good candidates in every odd dimension, such that the added conditions are few and simple, but when n is even, this is much trickier, as Euler himself noted when he tried to work it all out for $n=6$. His method is explained below.

Euler was one of the very great mathematicians of his century, and it may seem astonishing that as such, he would spend time on magic squares, if Benjamin Franklin's opinion is anything to go by. However, in light of the fact that Euler was not only very great, but very prolific, and produced many hundreds of articles on subjects as varied as shipbuilding, the motion of the moon, combinatorics, calculus as well as a popular science book called *Letters to a Princess of Germany.*

Euler suffered from poor eyesight and eyestrain from the age of 28, and at the age of 60 he became completely blind. Amazingly, half of his scientific work dates from after this date (the other half, dating from earlier in his life, having been produced while raising 13 children). In 1758, when he was 49, he solved a problem which, rumour has it, he heard talked about in a bar: if one places a knight on any square on a chessboard and uses only the knight's move, is it possible for the knight to visit every square on the chessboard once and only once? Basically, Euler would tackle any problem that came to his notice, so his magic-square paper is not that surprising after all!

Josep Maria Subirachs
The sculptor who created the façade of the Sagrada Familia temple in Barcelona, itself designed by Antonio Gaudi, inserted a rather peculiar magic square into one of the sculpted scenes. This square is based on Dürer's (rotated), but Subirachs replaced some of the numbers by one less.

1	14	14	4
11	7	6	9
8	10	10	5
13	2	3	15

The Subirachs square, Sagrada Familia, Barcelona

This causes repetition of the numbers 10 and 14 and elimination of 12 and 16, but the square remains magic; the magic constant is now 33. Subirachs made his square long after the age of Cornelius Agrippa, and the astrological symbolism attributed to the square has now become Christian symbolism. Thirty-three corresponds to the age of Christ at his death, and St Augustine, who underwent a religious epiphany through a river of tears while lying under a fig tree at the age of thirty-three devoted a quantity of speculation to the mystical meaning of that number.

Subirachs' design for the façade of the Sagrada Familia contains 16 scenes, laid out in a large 4-by-4 square reflecting the structure of the magic square, which is itself contained in the scene showing the kiss of Judas, sign of his betrayal. It is very possible that Subirachs included the magic square in this scene as a kind of talisman to conjure the evil and bad luck associated to the betrayal.

Creating Magic Squares

Many methods for creating magic squares have been developed over the last several centuries – yet it is known that none of these methods suffice to give *all* magic squares of a given size, nor is it even known how to make sure whether one has determined all of them (except for the smallest sizes, where every single possibility can be written down). Here, we describe only a few of the simplest and most charming methods.

Siamese Method for Odd Squares

There is a method to create diabolic squares of any size – as long as that size is an *odd number.* This method is attributed to Simon de la Loubère (1642–1729), a poet and diplomat born in Toulouse, France. He spent part of his career in Siam, and is rumoured to have learned his method from the locals. The method is quick and most satisfying, consisting of a stepping procedure and two simple rules.

Stepping procedure: Draw an n-by-n grid and place a 1 anywhere you like. Then place every successive number until n^2 in the box diagonally up to the right of the one you just filled in, subject to the following rules explaining what to do if you step outside of the grid:

Rule 1: If you step outside of the grid to any side (top, bottom, right, left), place your number in the opposite box of the row or column it would have been in, in other words in the leftmost box if you step out to the right, rightmost if you step out to the left, topmost if you step out to the bottom and bottommost if you step out to the top. If you step outside of the grid in the upper-right corner, place your number in the lower-left corner.

Rule 2: If you are about to place a number in a box which is already occupied, then place it directly below the number you previously filled in. If that makes you step outside the grid, apply rule 1.

Hey presto!

Interestingly, some of the starting positions for the initial 1 yield diabolic squares, others don't. Another mystery: which are the ones that work?

Euler's Method for Odd Squares

In a paper written in Latin and delivered to the St Petersburg Academy in 1776, the incredibly prolific and universal Swiss mathematician Leonhard Euler (1707–83) offered a method to construct magic squares of any dimension. His method, however, constitutes an actual algorithm only in the odd-dimensional case; the even-dimensional case seems to require some additional fumbling. The odd-dimensional solution, however, is delightful; closely related to the Siamese method, it contains it as a special case. The first step in the method consists in creating two squares: one containing the n letters $a_1, \dots, a_n$ (where ... represents the list of numbers between a_1 and a_n) each repeated n times, in such a way that each letter appears in each row and each column, and a second square having the same properties for the letters $b_1, \ldots, b_n$. Then one requires that the sum of the two squares has all the pairs $a_i + b_j$ with no repeated pairs.

Here is one very simple way of realising the two squares and their sum but, as Euler points out, there are many others.

a_1	a_2	a_3	a_4	a_5
a_2	a_3	a_4	a_5	a_1
a_3	a_4	a_5	a_1	a_2
a_4	a_5	a_1	a_2	a_3
a_5	a_1	a_2	a_3	a_4

b_1	b_1	b_1	b_1	b_1
b_2	b_2	b_2	b_2	b_2
b_3	b_3	b_3	b_3	b_3
b_4	b_4	b_4	b_4	b_4
b_5	b_5	b_5	b_5	b_5

a_1+b_1	a_2+b_1	a_3+b_1	a_4+b_1	a_5+b_1
a_2+b_2	a_3+b_2	a_4+b_2	a_5+b_2	a_1+b_2
a_3+b_3	a_4+b_3	a_5+b_3	a_1+b_3	a_2+b_3
a_4+b_4	a_5+b_4	a_1+b_4	a_2+b_4	a_3+b_4
a_5+b_5	a_1+b_5	a_2+b_5	a_3+b_5	a_4+b_5

Now one assigns the values $0, n, 2n, 3n, \ldots, (n-1)n$ to the numbers $a_1, \ldots, a_n$, but not necessarily in that order, and the values $1, 2, \ldots, n$ to the numbers b_n. Since the sum of every row and of every column is equal to the sum of all the a_i's – where a_i refers to any of the numbers a_1, a_2, a_3 etc – (which is equal to $(n^3-n^2)/2$) plus the sum of all the b_i's (which is $(n^2+n)/2$), the sum of every row and column is equal to $(n^3+n)/2$, which is the magic number. Thus automatically, whatever choice of assigning the values one makes, the row and column sums work out. To get the diagonals, one may need a special way of assigning values. For instance, in the example below, the sum of boxes on the main diagonal is the same as the sum and row columns, namely the sum of all the a_1's and all the b_1's, so it is automatically correct. But the sum of the boxes on the other diagonal is $na_n + b_1 + \ldots + b_n$ (where the ... refers to the sum of all the numbers between b_1 and b_n), so in order to get the right value, we need

$$na_n = a_1 + \ldots + a_n = (n^3 - n^2) / 2$$

which means that we must take

$$a_n = (n^2 - n) / 2 = (n(n-1)) / 2.$$

Whenever n is an odd number, (n-1) is even so (n-1)/2 is a whole number and n-(1/2)n is one of the possible values that can be assigned to a_n. For instance, when n=5 as in the above example, since (n-1)/2=2, we assign a_5=2.5=10, and a_1, a_2, a_3, a_4 can take the values 0, 5, 15, 20 in any order, while b_1, b_2, b_3, b_4, b_5 can take the values 1, 2, 3, 4, 5 in any order, and a magic square will always result.

However, when n is even, then n-1 is odd and n-1 is not divisible by 2. This means that there is no way to assign a possible value to a_n yielding a magic square, so our square above would not be magic for even n. However, as Euler showed, one can find other ways of disposing the a_1's and the b_1's that work in the even cases. However, there also exists a simple and direct algorithm to create even magic squares which we now explain.

Constructing Even Squares of Size Divisible by 4

An astonishing discovery was that the methods for creating magic squares of even size are *totally* different from constructing those of odd size! Instead of placing the numbers along slanted lines, these squares are essentially created by starting with a standard grid with the numbers filled out in order, and then switching certain pairs around symmetrically. Let us describe the most standard method for creating magic squares of size divisible by 4.

Step 1. Draw the n-by-n grid and write in all the numbers from 1 to n^2, starting from the upper-left corner and going row by row. Put boxes around the four n/4-by-n/4 boxes in the corners, and the n/2-by-n/2 sized centre box. The numbers inside these five boxes will be preserved.

1	2	3	4	5	6	7	8
9	10	11	12	13	14	15	16
17	18	19	20	21	22	23	24
25	26	27	28	29	30	31	32
33	34	35	36	37	38	39	40
41	42	43	44	45	46	47	48
49	50	51	52	53	54	55	56
57	58	59	60	61	62	63	64

Step 2. For every number in the upper half of the grid which is not inside a corner box or the central box, exchange it with the number diametrically opposite to it through the centre of the square; for instance 3 and 62, 12 and 53, 26 and 39, 33 and 32, 41 and 24. The result is magic!

1	2	62	61	60	59	7	8
9	10	54	53	52	51	15	16
48	47	19	20	21	22	42	41
40	39	27	28	29	30	34	33
32	31	35	36	37	38	26	25
24	23	43	44	45	46	18	17
49	50	14	13	12	11	55	56
57	58	6	5	4	3	63	64

There are obvious variants on this method consisting in starting in a different corner, moving left or right or up or down, etc. Another variant, using the version described above, is to take the n/2 middle columns and change their left-to-right order.

1	2	59	60	61	62	7	8
9	10	51	52	53	54	15	16
48	47	22	21	20	19	42	41
40	39	30	29	28	27	34	33
32	31	38	37	36	35	26	25
24	23	46	45	44	43	18	17
49	50	11	12	13	14	55	56
57	58	3	4	5	6	63	64

Clearly this operation does not change any of the row or column sums. In principle, it seems to risk altering the diagonal sums. However, a simple calculation shows that the sums of the elements of the two main diagonals of the inner $n/2$-by-$n/2$ square are equal (both equal to $n^3/4+n/4$). Therefore, writing the same columns in the opposite order does not change the total sum of these diagonals, and they can be reversed without spoiling the magic!

The Dürer magic square is obtained by this method. Start filling in a 4-by-4 grid by placing the 1 in the lower left-hand corner and then moving to the left. Then complete the switching procedure, and finish by exchanging the second and third columns.

Squares of Even Size not Divisible by 4

The method explained above only works if the size of the square is divisible by 4. The following method is based on it, but has to give special treatment to the extra two lines and columns that appear. Unlike the others, this method was developed only in the twentieth century – and the future will probably yield yet more new discoveries.

Step 1. Draw the n-by-n grid (here n=10) and divide it into boxes as in the following diagram. The regions labelled A, B (two regions considered as one) and C will play an important role on the next page.

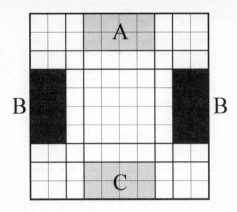

Step 2. Number the divided grid from 1 to n^2 starting in the upper left-hand corner and moving to the right (or more generally, starting in any corner, moving in any direction). But leave out all the numbers in the 'extra' two rows and columns.

1	2		4	5	6	7		9	10
11	12		14	15	16	17		19	20
31	32		34	35	36	37		39	40
41	42		44	45	46	47		49	50
51	52		54	55	56	57		59	60
61	62		64	65	66	67		69	70
81	82		84	85	86	87		89	90
91	92		94	95	96	97		99	100

Step 3. Exchange diametrically opposite numbers between regions A and C, and also between the two parts of region B, exactly as in the case where n is divisible by 4.

1	2		97	96	95	94		9	10
11	12		87	86	85	84		19	20
70	69		34	35	36	37		62	61
60	59		44	45	46	47		52	51
50	49		54	55	56	57		42	41
40	39		64	65	66	67		32	31
81	82		17	16	15	14		89	90
91	92		7	6	5	4		99	100

Step 4. Now we show how to deal with the extra lines and columns. First, place all the numbers of the left-hand missing column as they should be, but continue to leave out the two missing rows. Second, place the numbers of the right-hand missing column in the opposite up-down order to the way they should be (again leaving out the numbers which would appear in the rows).

1	2	3	97	96	95	94	98	9	10
11	12	13	87	86	85	84	88	19	20
70	69	33	34	35	36	37	68	62	61
60	59	43	44	45	46	47	58	52	51
50	49	53	54	55	56	57	48	42	41
40	39	63	64	65	66	67	38	32	31
81	82	83	17	16	15	14	18	89	90
91	92	93	7	6	5	4	8	99	100

Step 5. Now horizontally switch the numbers of these two columns which lie in the middle rows.

1	2	3	97	96	95	94	98	9	10
11	12	13	87	86	85	84	88	19	20
70	69	68	34	35	36	37	33	62	61
60	59	58	44	45	46	47	43	52	51
50	49	48	54	55	56	57	53	42	41
40	39	38	64	65	66	67	63	32	31
81	82	83	17	16	15	14	18	89	90
91	92	93	7	6	5	4	8	99	100

Step 6. And re-switch back just the single pair of numbers in those two columns which lie just below the middle of the grid.

1	2	3	94	95	96	97	98	9	10
11	12	13	87	86	85	84	88	19	20
70	69	68	34	35	36	37	33	62	61
51	52	58	44	45	46	47	43	59	60
50	49	53	54	55	56	57	48	42	41
40	39	38	64	65	66	67	63	32	31
81	82	83	17	16	15	14	18	89	90
91	92	93	7	6	5	4	8	99	100

Step 7. Now place the numbers in the two missing rows, as follows: write the expected numbers from *right to left* rather than from left to right, and leave out the four numbers at the intersection of the 'extra' rows and columns.

1	2	3	94	95	96	97	98	9	10
11	12	13	87	86	85	84	88	19	20
30	29		27	26	25	24		22	21
70	69	68	34	35	36	37	33	62	61
51	52	58	44	45	46	47	43	59	60
50	49	53	54	55	56	57	48	42	41
40	39	38	64	65	66	67	63	32	31
80	79		77	76	75	74		72	71
81	82	83	17	16	15	14	18	89	90
91	92	93	7	6	5	4	8	99	100

Step 8. Vertically switch the numbers from the extra rows that belong to the middle columns.

1	2	3	94	95	96	97	98	9	10
11	12	13	87	86	85	84	88	19	20
30	29		77	76	75	74		22	21
70	69	68	34	35	36	37	33	62	61
51	52	58	44	45	46	47	43	59	60
50	49	53	54	55	56	57	48	42	41
40	39	38	64	65	66	67	63	32	31
80	79		27	26	25	24		72	71
81	82	83	17	16	15	14	18	89	90
91	92	93	7	6	5	4	8	99	100

Step 9. Fill in the remaining four boxes with the numbers they would have contained in Step 1 if they had been filled in.

1	2	3	94	95	96	97	98	9	10
11	12	13	87	86	85	84	88	19	20
80	29	(23)	77	76	75	74	(28)	22	21
70	69	68	34	35	36	37	33	62	61
51	52	58	44	45	46	47	43	59	60
50	49	53	54	55	56	57	48	42	41
40	39	38	64	65	66	67	63	32	31
30	79	(73)	27	26	25	24	(78)	72	71
81	82	83	17	16	15	14	18	89	90
91	92	93	7	6	5	4	8	99	100

Finished! The result is an astonishing magic square!

Solutions to the Exercise Puzzles

The easy sudoku

8	4	9	3	2	5	6	7	1
6	3	2	7	1	9	4	8	5
5	7	1	6	8	4	3	2	9
7	8	3	1	5	6	2	9	4
2	9	6	4	7	8	5	1	3
4	1	5	9	3	2	7	6	8
1	5	4	8	6	7	9	3	2
3	2	7	5	9	1	8	4	6
9	6	8	2	4	3	1	5	7

The medium sudoku

3	8	2	5	7	9	4	1	6
4	1	5	6	3	8	9	2	7
6	7	9	4	2	1	8	5	3
5	4	7	8	9	3	2	6	1
1	2	8	7	4	6	5	3	9
9	6	3	1	5	2	7	8	4
8	9	4	3	1	5	6	7	2
7	3	6	2	8	4	1	9	5
2	5	1	9	6	7	3	4	8

The difficult sudoku

4	2	6	3	1	8	9	7	5
8	3	7	9	6	5	2	1	4
9	5	1	7	4	2	8	3	6
1	7	3	6	2	9	4	5	8
2	9	5	8	3	4	1	6	7
6	4	8	1	5	7	3	9	2
7	1	2	4	9	6	5	8	3
5	8	9	2	7	3	6	4	1
3	6	4	5	8	1	7	2	9

The even more difficult sudoku

3	1	5	7	2	6	4	9	8
8	4	2	3	1	9	6	7	5
9	7	6	8	4	5	3	1	2
5	9	8	1	6	3	2	4	7
4	2	3	9	7	8	5	6	1
7	6	1	2	5	4	9	8	3
2	3	9	4	8	1	7	5	6
1	5	4	6	3	7	8	2	9
6	8	7	5	9	2	1	3	4

The easy kakuro

The first medium kakuro

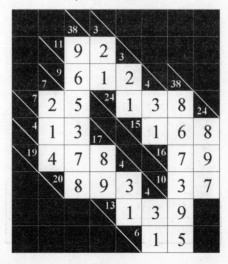

The second medium kakuro

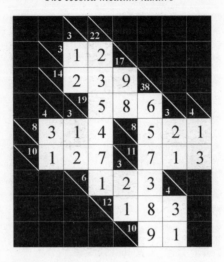

The difficult kakuro

The very difficult kakuro